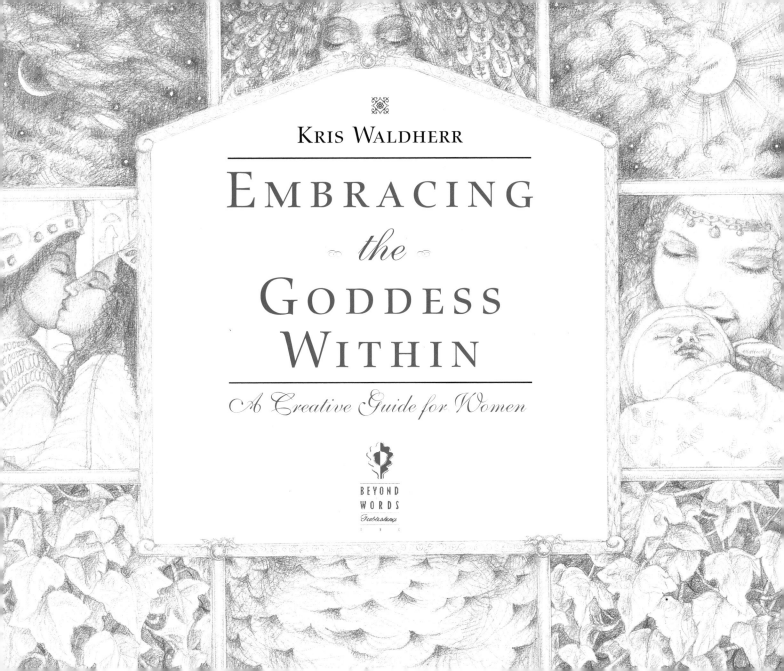

Kris Waldherr

EMBRACING

the

GODDESS

WITHIN

A Creative Guide for Women

BEYOND
WORDS
Publishing
INC

AGAIN, FOR TOM

My heartfelt thanks to Ellen Dreyer, Melanie Hope Greenberg, and Thomas Ross Miller for their help with this book. Special acknowledgment must also be given to the wonderful people at Beyond Words Publishing, Inc., especially Cindy Black, Richard Cohn, Lila Lee, Liz MacDonell, Marvin Moore, and Michelle Roehm. The beautiful typography and printing was overseen by Nancy Deahl and Leandra Jones — thank you also!

Beyond Words Publishing, Inc.
20827 N.W. Cornell Road, Suite 500
Hillsboro, Oregon 97124
503-531-8700
1-800-284-9673

Editor: Elizabeth MacDonell
Designer: Leandra Jones of Groove Jones Design
Production: Nancy Deahl
Proofreader: Marvin Moore

Printed in Singapore
Distributed to the book trade by Publishers Group West

Library of Congress Cataloging-in-Publication Data
Waldherr, Kris.
    Embracing the goddess within : a creative guide for women / Kris Waldherr.
      p.   cm.
    Includes bibliographical references and index.
    ISBN 1-885223-49-8
    1. Goddesses. 2. Women—Religious life. 3. Goddess religion. 4. Women and religion. I. Title.
BL473.5.W35 1997
291.2'114—dc21   97–497
                                                CIP

The corporate mission of Beyond Words Publishing, Inc.: *Inspire to Integrity*

CONTENTS

Introduction

SACRED STORIES, SACRED RITES

You are in all our great rites.
Who can understand you?

— ENHEDUANNA

WHEN ENHEDUANNA, A PRINCESS, high priestess, and celebrated poet, wrote these lines in 2300 B.C. to honor the great Sumerian goddess Inanna, could she have suspected that more than four thousand years later we would still be pondering this same question: How does one understand that transcendently feminine and powerful quality so many of us call *goddess*?

Embracing the Goddess Within is an exploration of this question as well as a tool for you to gain your own answers about what it means for us to embrace the goddess within. By "the goddess within," I am referring to that spirit often honored as the Divine Feminine — that nurturing, wise, and complex energy so many goddesses are shown to possess in abundance. Here are the sacred stories and myths of goddesses still honored, of goddesses significant at the dawn of humanity. Here also are their sacred rites, along with simple rituals and activities you can do to understand the goddess in her many names and forms.

Many of these goddess myths and rites reflect the beliefs of the peoples who created them. They tell us what was valued and revered, and in some cases even feared, in women. They show us the divine powers women have been imbued with forever. Our miraculous ability to create life from our bodies, our cycles of fertility that mirror the moon's waxing and waning have, from earliest times, connected us to the celestial realm and its magic.

One important form this connection took was in the worship by many cultures of a supreme triple goddess. This triple goddess, like the moon and her phases, reflected women's different stages of life: the waxing moon symbolizing the young girl; the full moon, the fertile woman; and finally the waning and dark moon, the post-menstrual woman often called the crone, who holds her "wise blood," or powers of creation, within herself. Some feminist scholars believe that later, as humans became more sophisticated in their needs, these three goddesses splintered into many goddesses — all of whom represented different parts of human life, all of whom made up the Divine Feminine.

One could call these goddesses and their qualities *archetypes,* or primordial symbols held deep within our psyches. As such, each of these goddess archetypes reveals the powers and talents women have. To acknowledge and honor these archetypes is a way for us to integrate all of these different qualities of the Divine Feminine into our lives — our creativities, strengths, and beauties, as well as our fears and angers.

Marie-Louise von Franz discusses the importance of accepting and understanding all of these qualities in her book *The Feminine in Fairy Tales.* Using the fairy tale of "Sleeping Beauty" as a point of departure, von Franz writes of the havoc wrought when a fairy godmother — or goddess — is not invited to the banquet celebrating the birth of the princess Briar Rose because there aren't enough gold plates. Since each of these goddesses represents qualities Briar Rose needs to live a full, happy life, the omission of one is tantamount to the refusal to accept all aspects of life, good and bad.

I agree with von Franz. To be healthy, complete women, we must accept all of our qualities. And since acceptance begins through understanding, to understand these goddess stories is a wonderful opportunity for us to accept ourselves as we are — not as society and the media tells us we should be. It is a chance for us to see our lives and our beauties anew with the eyes of a goddess. It is an opportunity for us to reclaim the Divine Feminine.

⟢ HOW TO USE THIS BOOK ⟢

Each goddess included within this book is presented by a retelling of her myth and an explanation of a ritual or activity to guide you toward connecting with the quality the goddess represents. The rituals in *Embracing the Goddess Within* have been taken from, or inspired by, traditional ceremonies and rites by which each goddess was honored. In this way, this book works on two levels: first, by presenting stories that in themselves offer wisdom, healing, and empowerment; secondly, by offering rituals that can show us ways of inviting the sacred into our lives.

In recent years, much has been written about the importance of stories and the sacred, healing properties they offer. The banquet of Briar Rose from "Sleeping Beauty" is an example of how a story's meaning can be expanded to help us better understand ourselves and the conditions in which we live. To fully understand a story is to fully possess it — and the myths of the goddesses are stories women especially need to possess. For these myths are *the* original women's stories. They are timeless. They reveal so much we need to hear about what it means to be strong, beautiful, and female in our world.

As you read these stories, notice any images that leap out and grab you, situations you may find yourself shaking your head in agreement with. These may be the places where the earthly meets the divine for you. Clarissa Pinkola Estes has said that "the flow of images in stories is medicine [and acts] like an antibiotic that finds the source of the infections and concentrates there. The story helps make that part of the psyche clear and strong again." If this is the case, then perhaps the goddess stories you particularly resonate with are ones that give you a special, sacred, healing "medicine" — a medicine which has been passed through many generations of women especially to you.

The goddess rituals also have been passed down to you through generations of women. Many feminist scholars agree that a great number of, if not most, women's festivals and rituals were occasions for honoring and acknowledging key passages of life. These gateways — whether they be first or last menstruation, the birth of a child or death of a member of the community, first love and marriage or the ending of a relationship — are common for women to this day. These goddess rituals serve to recognize our most important changes and tranformations. They tie us to our past and future, and help us honor our experiences and feelings.

By performing a ritual, we also are made to center ourselves and clarify our thoughts; in doing so, we allow room for the magical and mysterious to enter. This act of clarification forces us to confront our needs and desires. It allows us to take control of our lives, instead of feeling victimized by events we may think are outside our realm of power. In other words, rituals can help us learn what it means to be *self*-determined.

Perhaps most importantly, rituals are a way for us to embrace the divine. They can be a way to say yes to a particular goddess and her story. We embrace the goddess, and in embracing her, embrace ourselves — as the wise, empowered, wondrous women we all are.

The goddess stories and rituals are separated into six sections within this book, each of which highlights the needs and interests of the different stages of a woman's life. *Beginnings,* the book's first section, is about goddesses credited with the creation of the universe and explores our interconnection with the earth. The next sections, *Love* and *Motherhood,* focus on goddesses related to these areas. *Creativity* and *Strength* offer different ways women can experience their powers. Finally, *Transformations* presents goddesses associated with the crone, or post-menstrual, stage of our lives, as well as the ever-turning cycles of life and death. Also, other goddesses who share similar attributes are sometimes listed after each goddess ritual, but with a shorter description.

Obviously, each goddess is so much more than the characteristic she represents within this book. I hope that *Embracing the Goddess Within* will inspire you to read on to discover more about each goddess and the full experience that her story offers and has offered, in some cases, for thousands of years.

Toward that end, a bibliography is included at the end of this book, as well as a subject index listing the attributes and qualities of each goddess. Using this index, you can look up an attribute — such as motherhood or physical strength — and see which stories and rituals relate to this attribute.

Even though this book is written primarily for women, I hope that men will find in *Embracing the Goddess Within* the information needed to help them acknowledge their sacred feminine side. Since this book is intended as a creative tool for exploring the goddesses, each ritual can, and should, be seen as a point of departure for you to create your own personalized rituals — a wonderful way to connect with the Divine Feminine on an even more intimate level.

But now it is time for you to meet the goddess. She has been within you for many, many years and represents all the wisdoms and powers you could ever need, from the transcendent to the earthly, from the pragmatic to the fantastic. As in the story of the Sleeping Beauty, a glorious banquet is set before you, a banquet celebrating the Divine Feminine. But here there are plenty of golden plates for each goddess, so that all may be acknowledged and honored — and none left out.

And at this table also waits a gold plate for you too, goddess also.

One

BEGINNINGS

First in my prayer, before all other deities,
I call upon Gaia, Primeval Prophetess...
The Greek great earth mother.

— AESCHYLUS

What — or who — could have created the mysterious, infinite complexity of connectiveness we call the universe? How did it all begin "once upon a time"? In this section, our exploration centers on some of the goddesses credited with creating the earth and universe as we know it. It is here that the Divine Feminine is perhaps at her most powerful and all-encompassing.

Gaia, the Greek goddess, was said to have made the universe from her womb, while the Egyptian goddess Hathor was invoked as the Celestial Cow, capable of creating milk to nourish all of her dependent creations. The Norse goddess Erda fed the great World Tree, named Yggdrasil, with the water of wisdom from her divine fountain, located at the earth's center. Finally, the Native American divinity Spider Woman was believed to have created the web of life with her thoughts, and human beings from balls of differently colored clay and soil.

Like the creation goddesses acknowledged here, as women we are all creatresses; all life issues from us. As such, we reflect the universe within ourselves and our bodies. Using this equation, is it any wonder so many goddesses are believed to be the Great Mother?

Gaia

CELESTIAL CREATION

WHAT COULD HAVE EXISTED BEFORE Gaia, the earth? It is difficult to imagine — our minds and senses are irrevocably intertwined with all of our experiences of life upon this earth. The beauty of our green and blue planet with its many animals, plants, and other forms of life has a magnificence that warrants our respect and protection.

Gaia is the name of the goddess with which the ancient Greeks honored our earth. A cosmic, procreative womb which emerged out of the primeval void called Chaos, it was believed Gaia existed before all other life. Gaia formed from her womb the sky, which she called Uranus, to keep her company and to make love with. Sky lying upon Earth created numerous children within Gaia's great womb, but Uranus, fearful they would prove stronger than he, would not allow Gaia to give birth to them. However, Gaia gave her strongest child Kronos, or Time, a sickle made of a steely diamondlike material called adamontine, which he used to cut Uranus's genitals from the portal of her womb.

In this way Gaia created all the gods and goddesses of the Greek world. At her famed shrine at Delphi, Gaia was especially worshipped by priestesses who threw sacred herbs into a cauldron, using the fragrant smoke to invoke Gaia's eternal wisdom.

❋

☙ RITUAL FOR GAIA ☙
Celebrating Creation — A Guided Meditation

Guided meditation is perhaps the simplest form of ritual. All you need are a receptivity to creating a quiet space within yourself and a willingness to allow the mysterious to take place. Often when the word *meditation* is used, it brings to mind elaborate methods of breathing and long periods of time sitting in uncomfortable positions. Fortunately, it doesn't have to be that way; a meditation can be as simple as closing your eyes and stilling your thoughts long enough to feel the inner center of your being, that part of yourself which is constant and perfect. Guided meditations are one way to structure an experience within this space.

Find a comfortable place to sit in a quiet room where you know you won't be disturbed. A softly lit room is nice, especially if it's glowing with candles; candlelight is a good way to define the passage between our everyday existence and a more primordial one, where fire was used for light instead of electricity. Within this space, allow yourself to forget about all your concerns of the day. By this act of consciously separating yourself from your ordinary life, you have rendered your space *sacred*, a word whose root means "set apart from."

When you are settled into your sacred space, take a good look at everything around you. What do you see? For example, look out your window and take note of the time of day or night, the placement of the sun or moon, the time of year, the weather. Now close your eyes and listen to what you hear. Depending on where you live, you may hear a singing bird or children playing. If you live in a city you may hear horns honking or car alarms blaring. Regardless, let all the sounds you hear begin to fade away as you begin to notice the sound of your breath.

Finally, notice what you feel. Is the place where you are sitting hard or soft? What does the fabric of your clothing or upholstered furniture feel like against your skin? Allow all these sensations to fade away also as you go within to that deepest, core part of yourself.

Within yourself, consider Gaia's story. What must it have been like to create the universe from her celestial womb? Like Gaia, as women most of us have the capacity to create life within ourselves. Try to remember the first time you became aware of the seasons of the year, all the creation of Gaia: Do you remember your first snowfall or sweltering summer night when even your skin was too hot to touch? When did you first notice that life was broken into the two parts, one ruled by sun and the other by stars and moon? As you think back, consider the cycles of our Earth, other planets, the sun, and the cosmos, and know that by honoring them with your attention you are as much creatress as Gaia. When you are ready, open your eyes.

∽ OTHER GODDESSES ∽

ADITI ∽ In India, the goddess Aditi is believed to be the creator of life. Because she gave birth to the planets and stars, she is often honored with the title of Mother Space.

Erda

INTERCONNECTED LIFE

ERDA, OR URD, THE NORSE earth goddess, was believed to live in a cave within the deepest recesses of the earth by the roots of Yggdrasil, the vast World Tree whose limbs sustained and connected all of life, and around whose roots the earth revolved on its axis. It was from this shadowy cave, where rich soil met hungry root, that Erda's plentiful fountain of wisdom watered the World Tree. This magical spring of water enabled Yggdrasil to grow so great that its tallest branches reached the heavens and its widest gave shade to all.

Erda was invoked by those in need of her all-knowing wisdom as well as for aid in bending the inexorable powers of fate, over which she ruled. One myth tells the story of how the Norse god Odin gave up one of his eyes for the privilege of drinking from Erda's fountain; his ceaseless, ambitious quest for wisdom and control over fate was worth far more to him than the pedestrian gift of eyesight.

Another story claims that Erda is the oldest goddess of the three Norns, a trio of sister goddesses believed to rule over the past, present, and future.

❧ RITUAL FOR ERDA ❧
Divining Fate — An Oracle

To the Norse, because of Erda's association with fate, there was a clear connection between the goddess and the art of divination, a valued part of pre-Christian Scandinavian society. It may be hard to imagine today, but at that time every home was open to seeresses, female practitioners of the art of divination, who were believed to receive help from the spirit world. The predictions presented by the seeress often came in the form of mysterious poems obtained by the use of runes or other oracles whose messages the seeress was skilled in understanding.

The seeress made her runes from bone or stripes of wood cut from a nut-bearing tree. Upon these runes she carved or painted potent symbols. In a way, by this act of making runes from a tree, the seeress was drawing from that same fountain of wisdom Erda used to nurture Yggdrasil, the World Tree — and, consequently, invoking Erda.

Using natural forms as oracles also reminds us that Nature can give us the answers we need to our most urgent and primal questions. Like those Scandinavian seeresses of long past, you could make runes of your own and paint them with symbols that are meaningful to you. Runes can also be made using objects such as eagle feathers, rocks, curled pieces of bark, oak leaves, or other objects that have special meaning to you.

If all your runes are shaped the same, place each rune face down upon a flat surface and look up to the sky. If you have a specific question to ask of the runes, now is the time to do so. Or you could trust that the information you receive will be what you need. As you touch each rune, see if any one feels as if it is pressing itself into your hand. Choose it and look down upon it. How does this rune speak to your condition?

If the runes are different enough that you could recognize them by touch, place them within a cloth bag. Give the bag a little shake and spill the runes gently out. Can you read a story from the pattern the runes fall into? What does it tell you?

Another oracle used by the Norse for divination was the earth itself. This method depends on our acknowledging Nature as a living, wise being who coexists with us. The Norse used many aspects of Nature as oracles — animals, birds, the sky, and the ocean. They thought that the observation of these things could bring answers to questions posed. Horses, in particular, were considered to be confidants of the gods and goddesses, able to reveal heaven's will to sensitive humans. A horse's calm movements could promise a peaceful solution to the question posed, whereas other movements could mirror other outcomes.

To consult the sea, wade knee-deep into its depths and shout out your question. Notice the waves' reaction: Do they splash up in affirmation? Do they lap peacefully? Consider also the color and hue of the water: Is the water clear or muddy? Blue or bloody-brown? What sounds do you hear? The sky could be consulted in a similar manner as well.

All these factors make up the language of the earth. Take note of the wisdom you've received from Erda, Mother Earth, and thank her for her answer.

∽ OTHER GODDESSES ∽

DANU ∽ Honored in ancient Ireland as the greatest and wisest of all Celtic goddesses, Danu is considered to be the mother of all the gods and goddesses. She provides her followers with prosperity as well as knowledge.

Hathor

THE PROMISE OF PLENTY

AS THE GODDESS OF FERTILITY and plenty, Hathor was honored in ancient Egypt as the Golden One — a divinity powerful enough to help her worshippers with dilemmas ranging from the lack of prosperity to love.

Believed to be the Egyptian mother of the gods and goddesses, Hathor was also called the Celestial Cow because of her ability to nurture the entire world. Not surprisingly, the goddess was often depicted with the face of a cow or wearing a headdress of horns with a circle, symbolizing the sun, resting above them. Public festivals to Hathor were held in November. These rituals often consisted of the ceremonial carrying and displaying of the sacred statues of the Celestial Cow. Many also identify the Celestial Cow with the Milky Way, that beautiful band of stars so visible on dark, moonless nights.

Hathor was so popular that at one point she was served by as many as sixty-one priestesses in her sacred temple. Even today her ancient shrines are visited by women seeking her assistance with the conception of children.

❋

❧ RITUAL FOR HATHOR ❧

Invoking the Golden One — An Abundance Ritual

From the earliest times, Hathor was petitioned for help in creating abundance personally (such as help with a love affair) as well as communally (a generous agricultural harvest to feed everyone). What would you like Hathor to help you grow? Use these ancient rituals to create your own offering to Hathor, the bringer of plenty.

One ritual involved cows led out to fields and milked, their new milk then poured upon the hungry ground as libations to the goddess. This ritual would be performed in hopes of persuading Hathor to send nurturing rain to help the crops grow. These acts were done in hopes of creating *sympathetic magic*, this being the belief that an action performed on a smaller scale to the hoped-for outcome can create it by magically reflecting it — as above, so below. A similar but simpler ritual performed by the Egyptians to please Hathor used magically charged water, which was sprinkled upon the earth.

To help fertilize your own dreams of abundance, take a golden candle to invoke the Golden One. With a pointed object, carve upon its surface your name and what it is that you desire Hathor's help with. Place the candle in a safe place and light it. Now take a bowl of clear water and bless the water by plunging the burning candle into it, like the Egyptians did so many thousands of years ago. Then sprinkle the sanctified water onto the earth. Know that as you do so you are placing your hopes out in the world.

For three nights after performing this ritual, light your candle to Hathor and think about what you have requested — and what you can do to help her help you make your wish come true.

Spider Woman

THE WEB OF LIFE

MANY CULTURES AROUND THE WORLD during many different times have believed that all the aspects of the world are connected together by a strong but delicately woven web. The Pueblo Indians credit the spinning of this web of life to a creation goddess so potent that her true name is never spoken. Many call this goddess Spider Woman; because everything was created from her thoughts, she is also called Thought Woman.

Spider Woman existed before the world existed. But by spinning and chanting, she was able to create the four directions of the universe: north, south, east, and west. From within this space, she produced her daughters, Ut Set and Nau Ut Set. Following their mother's directions, Ut Set and Nau Ut Set made the sun, moon, and stars to banish darkness from the universe, using shells, turquoise, red rock, yellow stone, and clear crystal to create them.

As she spun her web and thought, Spider Woman made all of life — the mountains, lakes, oceans, and deserts. She created human beings from differently colored clays. And finally, using a last thread of her web, Spider Woman connected us to her always.

❖

❧ RITUAL FOR SPIDER WOMAN ❧
Opening the Door — A Group Chant

Merlin Stone, a feminist scholar, writes in her book *Ancient Mirrors of Womanhood* that each of us has a "doorway" at the top of our head that joins us to Spider Woman. In yogic traditions, this doorway is called the crown chakra, a place of energy associated with the highest spiritual enlightenment. To invoke the creative wisdom of Spider Woman, all we need to do is open our doorway and take note of that precious thread connecting us to her web.

Hopefully, you know what it feels like to be truly engrossed in something creative, to lose track of time — those moments when we have felt blessed by our sense of connection with the universe. These moments could have been a time when your doorway to Spider Woman's wisdom was open. Perhaps all that was needed was to recognize her gift for what it was.

Like Spider Woman as she spun her web, one way to open your doorway is with music or chanting. This technique has been used by shamans around the globe to bring about a transcendental state of mind. In Siberia, the shaman straddled his or her ceremonial drum and beat it as if it were a steed transporting them to the place of the spirits. Many Native American traditions also include ceremonial drumming and chants as a means of reaching this heightened state of consciousness.

Drumming and chanting are wonderful group rituals to participate in, whether or not you are musically inclined. By gathering a group of women together to invoke Spider Woman, you are also honoring your connections to them and the world; indeed, you are honoring your own web of life, which you have created. In past times, women often came together to keep company as they wove and sewed the clothes needed to garb their families. These gatherings were seen as times of power, for it was during them that women forged and honored their relationships with each other. You can do the same in your gathering.

Chants for your group event to honor Spider Woman could be taken from any number of sources. As a group, you could write one. Or you could choose one from a book. One book I particularly like, Barbara Walker's *Women's Rituals: A Sourcebook*, has many good chants within its pages for you to draw from. If you feel too shy about creating your own music to open your doorway, you could listen to a tape of Native American music or any music with a beat strong enough to get caught up in.

As you chant or sing or drum, feel the sound vibrating up through your body, up to the top of your head where your doorway to Spider Woman lies. See if you can feel the music go through it, into the universe, toward the creative wisdom of Spider Woman.

∽ OTHER GODDESSES ∽

BERCHTA ∽ Berchta, the German goddess who spins the thread of destiny, is said to wear a mantle of snow upon her shoulders. She also presides over household affairs.

BILIKU ∽ In the Andaman Islands in India, the creation goddess Biliku often appears in the form of a spider. Considered to be both benevolent and malevolent, Biliku was believed to be the first deity to own and control fire.

Two

LOVE

In that meadow where horses have grown glossy,
and all spring flowers grow wild,
the anise shoots fill the air with aroma.
And there our queen Aphrodite pours
celestial nectar in the gold cups.

— SAPPHO

Persephone and her first love. Aphrodite's passion and sensuality. Benzai-ten's serene, transcendent love that questions nothing. Seductive, flirtatious, noble, beautiful, warm, and cool — all-goddess , all-divine, all-knowing of heartbreak and joy without end.

As there are experiences of passionate love, so there are goddesses to reflect our experiences. Presented here within the grand movement of our changing relationships as we grow in maturity and wisdom, these goddesses reflect our growth from girl to woman, waxing moon to full.

The story of Persephone, Greek goddess of the underworld, offers us a chance to explore the often difficult transition from virgin to bride. The Aztec goddess Xochiquetzal and the celestial Aphrodite reveal sexual pleasure's siren song, while

Hera extends the structure of marriage to these powerful forces. The Japanese goddess Benzai-ten shows us the wisdom of knowing, accepting, and loving our partners as they are.

How fortunate for us that the passage of time allows us chances to savor different types of love relationships. Whether they are with a lover, partner, or spouse, short-term or lasting through eternity, all love relationships offer joys and challenges — as we yearn toward the wedding of the Divine Feminine to her beloved consort.

Persephone

✦

FIRST BLOOD, FIRST LOVE

THE MYSTERIOUS, DARK MYTH OF the Greek goddess Persephone is in many ways the story of a girl's initiation into the meaning of her own blood — the menstrual blood that holds the secret of sexual ripening. Few women are emotionally ready to be sexually active at the time of their first flow; it is this first blood, however, that shows that this time is not far off. Soon we will fall in love with another and choose to share our bodies with this person.

Persephone was the beloved daughter of the harvest goddess Demeter, but she was forced to become the wife of Pluto, ruler of the underworld. He had fallen in love with her and, as she bent to pluck a narcissus, abducted the girl from a meadow. While in the underworld, Persephone ate nothing but six seeds of the pomegranate, an act that showed Persephone's reluctant acceptance of her sexuality as well as of Pluto as her husband. This act also ensured her separation from her mother for half of the year — a month for each seed tasted.

With its many clustered seeds, the pomegranate is a rich allegory for the fruitfulness of a woman's ovaries; indeed, many paintings from the Renaissance portray the Virgin Mary with pomegranates, to show her life-giving force. Persephone's sojourn into the underworld can also represent for some women the dark, depressive underworld of their psyche, a place many do not encounter until sexual maturity.

❖

∽ RITUAL FOR PERSEPHONE ∽

The Eleusinian Mysteries — A Celebration, An Initiation

The miraculous power of first menstruation is something our society has few rituals to commemorate, though other less industrialized cultures do. Like Persephone's descent into the sunless underworld, these initiation rituals usually included the segregation of the menstruating women to a hut used solely for this purpose; no light was allowed to enter its darkened interior. Men, having no equivalent to menstruation, often created rituals to mirror what happens naturally to women. Tribes in Australia knock out a boy's tooth at puberty, creating a bleeding mouth; other cultures practiced subcision, an operation that splits the penis lengthwise to resemble a vulva.

The main rituals associated with Persephone are the great Eleusinian mysteries. Though some believe at one time the mysteries allowed only women as participants, little is known of these secret rites. One thing is certain, however: Those who underwent the rites of Eleusis were changed irrevocably. Cicero wrote of them, "We have been given a reason not only to live in joy, but also to die with better hope."

The Eleusinian mysteries took place every September in Athens. They began with the initiates fasting for nine days. At the end of this time, they purified themselves in the ocean and proceeded by foot onto Eleusis, a walk that took most of the day. Once there, the initiates' eyes were covered with cloth and they were brought into the temple.

Little is known after this. Some say that the blindfolded initiates were led through mazelike passageways; others think they were shown a sheaf of grain, which represented Persephone's return from the underworld as well as Demeter's miraculous life-creating powers. When the initiates were led back to the world of light, they broke their fast with *kykeon*, a drink of water and mint thickened by meal.

To honor a young girl's first menstruation (if she is comfortable enough with her body to allow it without embarrassment), a celebration could be held to welcome the young girl into the community of women, using elements from the Eleusinian mysteries. The new woman being honored wears a dress as red as the rich blood of life, and a crown made of grain sheaves upon her brow. To break the fast, serve a cake made with flour and mint, the same ingredients in the kykeon drunk by the initiates at Eleusis.

Finally, within a room as dark as the underworld, recount the story of Persephone (or use a reading from a book such as my own *Persephone and the Pomegranate* or Christine Downing's *The Long Journey Home: Re-visioning the Myth of Demeter and Persephone for Our Time*) as a pomegranate is nibbled and passed from woman to woman, demonstrating the miracle of blood which binds us together.

☙ OTHER GODDESSES ☙

FORTUNA VIRGINENSIS ☙ Fortuna Virginensis is an aspect of Fortuna, the Roman goddess of luck. Newly married women honored her with offerings of their garments after their bridal night.

Xochiquetzal

❁

UNDERSTANDING LOVE'S POWER

REPUTED TO BE PLAYFUL, MERRY, and beautiful — as well as extremely flirtatious — Xochiquetzal, the Aztec goddess of love and beauty, was desired by many men who attempted to win her away from her husband, Tlaloc, the rain god. Many poems found upon manuscripts from this era sing praises of her loveliness, her gaiety, and her seductive, regal presence.

Like the Greek goddess Persephone, Xochiquetzal was believed to be a young maiden; unlike Persephone, Xochiquetzal was fully aware of the powers of her sexuality and their effect upon the opposite sex. She used them often for her amusement and pleasure.

Xochiquetzal was also honored as the goddess of flowers, dance, music, and crafts, aspects of life that are useful as well as pleasurable. Her flower-laden garden rested upon a mountaintop above the nine heavens, a paradise where devotees to Xochiquetzal were certain they would be united with the goddess after their earthly lives had ended.

❖

❧ RITUAL FOR XOCHIQUETZAL ❧
The Goddess and the Marigold — An Appreciation Exercise

Some anthropologists believe that festivals to honor Xochiquetzal contained rituals that introduced the young to sexual pleasures in a safe environment. Today, with the tragic scourge of AIDS and other sexually transmitted diseases, young women especially need to approach the intoxication of sex and love carefully.

Perhaps an Aztec manuscript from the era of Xochiquetzal expresses this best. Within it a parent advises his daughter, "Understand that you are noble. See that you are very precious, even while you are still only a little lady. You are a turquoise ... you are a descendant of noble lineage...." We would do well to listen to this admonition. Like the recipient of this advice, like Xochiquetzal, we are *all* descendants of noble lineage, we are *all* divine; we need to treat our sexuality — and its powers — as divine also.

Xochiquetzal's name means "feather flower," an appropriate name for a goddess whose sacred flower is the marigold, a flower with many feathery petals. It has the subtle, complex, multipetaled power of a woman's sexuality.

For this exercise, you need a marigold and paper and pencil. Sit in a quiet, softly lit room where you are comfortable. Close your eyes.

Imagine you are sitting in sunlight so brilliant that you can see its red heat through your closed eyelids. As you do so, feel the sensual heat; see if you can feel Xochiquetzal's presence within you. How does her flirtatious, seductive presence feel to you? Ask what you need to do to feel that energy as part of yourself more often. Once you receive your answer, open your eyes and write it down.

Now pick up your marigold. Look at its tightly curled petals closely: Can you look

at only one petal at a time? As you consider each petal, write down an aspect of feminine sexuality that you appreciate. If you feel uncomfortable with this, give yourself time. You may need to think about it and come back to this exercise, but chances are there are more aspects to appreciate than there are petals on the flower!

When you have finished, place your list and your marigold under your pillow. Let your list seep into your subconscious as you sleep, empowering you and your sexual relationships.

∽ OTHER GODDESSES ∽

LALITA ∽ In India, this youthful goddess of love and sex amuses herself by playing with the universe like a flirtatious woman with her lover. Appropriately, Lalita's name translates as "the amorous."

OSHUN ∽ The Yoruba goddess Oshun is as flirtatious and sparkling as the river that bears her name. Her exotic beauty is intoxicating: her dark skin as sleek as velvet, her elaborate headdress made of richly hued feathers to set off her brilliant eyes. Worshipped in both Africa and the Caribbean, Oshun is a popular goddess for those wishing to attract love.

Aphrodite

ROMANTIC LOVE

QUEEN OF BEAUTY, QUEEN OF love — to many, the goddess Aphrodite is the embodiment of these intoxicating, maddening forces. Her powerful realm includes the ecstasies and pleasures, the smiling torments that arise from romantic love. No human can escape the grasp of her seductive influence — nor would we want to.

Known to the Romans as Venus, the Greek goddess Aphrodite was fashioned from sea and foam, and brought to earth in a conch shell; indeed, Aphrodite's name translates literally as "she who comes from the foam." Her attendants, three Graces named Joyous, Brilliance, and Flowering, show the wonders the goddess can offer, if she chooses to smile upon our earthly petitions. Wherever Aphrodite walks, flowers rise from the earth to welcome her rejuvenative gifts. All humans and animals are inspired to love each other, thus assuring the continuation of life.

As the unwilling wife of Hephaestus, or Vulcan, the lame god of forging and handicrafts, Aphrodite serves to represent the necessary balance of beauty with utilitarianism. But a goddess of such overwhelming beauty and sensuality could not be loyal to one so ugly; many were those whom the goddess favored with the gift of her love.

❈

∞ RITUAL FOR APHRODITE ∞
Romancing the Goddess — Love Magic

Images of sensuality and romance abound in Aphrodite's myths. On the island of Cyprus, where the goddess was believed to first set foot upon the earth, shellfish were sacred due to their similiar shape to a woman's vulva. The rose, Aphrodite's special flower, was the object of desire in medieval quest romances, understood to really mean the velvety, rosy folds of a woman's most precious jewel.

The scent of myrtle, also sanctified to Aphrodite, bespoke of love and attraction; brides of the Greco-Roman world wore wreaths of it on their wedding day. Ovid writes that Aphrodite, as Venus, was worshipped by women at the Veneralia, a festival celebrated every year on April first. For this holiday, Ovid claimed, women must "wash the statues of Venus all over, put their golden necklaces on again and give them roses and other flowers; and then, as the goddess commands, you must wash yourself under the green myrtle."

But it was Cestus, Aphrodite's richly embroidered girdle or belt, that held the goddess's most powerful spell. This magical length of cloth could make the wearer seductive enough to bewitch even the most unyielding of lovers into romantic congress.

Many of these stories can easily be seen in our courtship rituals today. Instead of worshipping conch shells, we feed our lovers oysters and whisper to them about the quickening of sexual prowess. We bring roses for Valentine's Day. We scent ourselves with sweet perfumes, and we dress with special care to look our most enchanting.

To invoke Aphrodite's presence within yourself, you could ready yourself for your lover by performing this love spell.

Bathe in salted water scented with roses, like the ocean bath from which Aphrodite was formed. Since six is considered the sacred number of the goddess of love, six candles set around the rim of your bathtub could help focus your attention for the upcoming night of bliss. As you soak, imagine that the water is a sacred fluid imbuing you with the powers of Aphrodite.

As you dry yourself, feel your flesh absorb the rose water, leaving you with the subtle perfume of the goddess. Then, before you dress, take a moment to close your eyes and visualize your garments. Imagine them glowing with a pinkish golden light. This light is the power of Cestus, Aphrodite's magical girdle. As you dress, feel Cestus's warm, earthy, seductive light all around you.

If you wish, you could buy or make a special embroidered belt to wrap around your waist. Like Cestus, it would serve to represent the irresistible force of your attraction and should be worn only for — and taken off by — your adored one.

∞ OTHER GODDESSES ∞

RATI ∞ Worshipped in both Bali and India, this beautiful goddess often is said to appear as a ripe, pregnant woman with full breasts that promise pleasure and milk. Rati is the giver of passionate nights, of soulful kisses returned. She is one of the wives of Kama, the god of love.

Benzai-ten

❖

To Know the Beloved

In many romantic relationships, once the first infatuation of love begins its necessary turn toward reality, it may feel as though the spell of desire has been broken. We no longer know our beloved. Like Beauty in "Beauty and the Beast," we cannot recognize the prince for the beast he seems to be. But Benzai-ten, the only goddess among the seven Japanese gods of happiness, can help us see past our disillusionment into the true inner heart of love.

In addition to being a marriage goddess, Benzai-ten is also a goddess of literature, music, and wealth. Believed to be the daughter of a dragon king, Benzai-ten agreed to wed a ferocious, child-devouring dragon in exchange for his promise to stop eating them. Upon their marriage, the dragon lost his appetite for children; his love for the goddess and her acceptance of him had healed his "beastly" temperament.

Like Beauty, Benzai-ten's acceptance of her dragon-husband shows us women's ability to recognize and accept true love, even when it comes in unexpected packages. Perhaps it is for this reason that Benzai-ten is believed to help young lovers come together. Since she is the goddess of romantic happiness, devotees of this lovely goddess will often leave letters upon her shrines to implore her aid.

❁

⌒ RITUAL FOR BENZAI-TEN ⌒
The Scarlet Thread — A Love Ritual

Another story about Benzai-ten tells how she acted as a go-between for a couple who had never met. While visiting a temple to Benzai-ten, a young man noticed a piece of rice paper floating from the air to rest at his feet. Written upon the delicate sheet was a love poem, one that spoke to his heart. The exquisite calligraphy suggested a feminine hand; immediately the young man knew he had to find the writer and marry her. But how could he do this? Deciding the goddess would take pity upon his mad quest, the young man resolved to pray at her shrine every night for a week.

At the end of his last evening at Benzai-ten's shrine, just as the dark sky had softened to azure and the young man was about to leave, an elderly man walked in. He knotted one end of a scarlet thread around the young man's wrist; the other end he placed as an offering into the temple fire. As the old man extinguished the flame, a young woman entered the temple. With skin as pale as the rice moon and hair as black as the starless night, she was as enchanting as that love poem had been.

"Benzai-ten has been moved by your prayers," the elderly man announced to the younger. "Now, come meet your bride." And he explained that the beautiful woman was the writer of the calligraphy that had so intoxicated the young man. The two recognized one another as true mates and were wed, blessed by the generosity of Benzai-ten.

Like the young couple in this story, you could ask Benzai-ten to help you recognize your true mate — the one who is tied to you by a scarlet thread.

The scarlet thread is a common motif in many Japanese folktales, and is believed to bind a couple destined to be together; this thread between the two is as unbreakable as fate itself. Whether we are in a committed relationship or searching for one, many times it is not easy to recognize who is at the other end of our scarlet thread. Instead, we see it tied to our beliefs of how things should be.

To help you recognize your true mate, take a sheet of rice paper and your favorite pen. On a night three days before the full moon, shut yourself away with paper and pen. Upon this sheet of paper, write, "I ask for this or anything better in my true mate."

Before you fill in your list of desirables, take a moment to be still with your thoughts about what you want. Take note of your reactions as you write down each item. If you feel any resistance, *stop*. Maybe what you think you want isn't right for you. Or maybe you're not quite ready for love — nothing to be ashamed of, but something that should be acknowledged. Remember, by including the phrase "or anything better," you are giving Benzai-ten permission to intercede on your behalf and make sure you meet the right partner. All you need to do is to be receptive.

Finally, when you've finished writing your list, remember to thank the higher power that will help you recognize your true love when the time is right. Do not tell anyone what you are doing; you will only weaken your ritual by speaking of it.

For the next three nights, read your list to yourself. Then, on the night of the full moon, fold your list into a small square. Take a scarlet thread — the same thread Benzai-ten uses to bind us to our true loves — and wrap the square several times with it, so you cannot peek at your list. Now put your list away in a secret spot and try to forget about it. By doing so, you are allowing room for the magical to occur.

Hera

For Better or Worse

THE GODDESS HERA WAS HONORED as the goddess of marriage in ancient Greece. As ruler of this sacred state, she is responsible for its protection; her anger when the bonds of matrimony were not respected is perhaps as legendary as her difficult, tempestuous relationship with her husband, Zeus. He was as notoriously unfaithful to the goddess as she was faithful to him. Hera's anger at Zeus was often expressed in the form of storms as violent as their domestic squabbling.

To win Hera as his bride, Zeus courted her for three hundred years upon the island of Samos, the goddess's birthplace. Frustrated by his lack of success, he transformed himself into a cuckoo. Hera, charmed by the bird, allowed it into her lap, where Zeus took back his natural form and seduced her.

Sacred to Hera are the pomegranate and lily — two potent symbols of fertility and femininity seen in many cultures around the world — as well as oxen, trees, and mountains. Ancient rituals to Hera usually involved the use of these elements in some way or form.

❖

∞ RITUAL FOR HERA ∞
The Joiner of Marriage — The Wedding Ceremony

As Hera Zygeia, or Hera the Joiner, Hera presided over marriage ceremonies as well as guarded the union itself. Her uneasy relationship with Zeus also parallels the expectations we bring into the marriage relationship, for better *and* for worse. Wedding rituals especially are so rich in feminine symbolism that it is easy to recognize the influence of the Divine Feminine. By participating in them, we cannot help but embody the goddess within ourselves. Use these symbols and rituals to add meaning to your own wedding ceremonies.

The bride, dressed in her white gown, reminds us of the beauty of the moon, that most feminine of heavenly bodies. The honeymoon, referring to the lunar, menstrual month, is the moon of sensuality and love. Breaking the wine glass, a potent part of the Jewish wedding ceremony, represents the breaking of the maiden's hymen, the spilling of her virgin blood. The glass or cup shared by the newlywed couple represents the womb, in which magical blood and nurturing waters bring new life into form. The placing of a golden ring upon the third left finger derives from the medieval belief that a vein ran directly from that finger to the heart. It also symbolizes the placement of the penis into the circle of the vagina.

In pagan wedding ceremonies, called handfastings, the partners' hands are bound together with a knotted cord, the knot symbolizing eternity and union as well as the intertwining web of life that binds us together. This practice dates back to ancient Sumerian wedding rites. In your wedding ritual, you could use a golden cord to symbolically bind the two of you together in life and love.

Instead of seating your guests in rows, you could say your vows surrounded by a circle of family and friends. Pagan rites are often carried out within a sacred circle cast by the priest or priestess. The circle here represents the continuity of life, without beginning or end.

Hera's wedding to Zeus was celebrated in Boeotia with a ritual utilizing symbols of the god and goddess. A piece of wood was carried to a shed in a cart drawn by oxen and set on fire; since oxen and trees were sacred to Hera, and Zeus ruled over fire and lightning, the correlation is clear. In many ways, this ritual is tainted with traditional expectations of marriage: The male energy, symbolized by fire, devours the passive feminine — just as marriages were originally arranged for the sake of political or material alliances, the women little more than possession or slave.

Happily, the wedding ceremony has changed over time to reflect a more equitable relationship between men and women. It is perhaps one of the most significant rituals that a woman can partake in, taking us from one stage of life into the next — the magical, alchemic transformation of "me into we."

∽ OTHER GODDESSES ∽

ARUNDHATI ∽ In India, this goddess, whose name means "fidelity," is called upon in marriage ceremonies. Arundhati is the wife of Dharma and is often depicted upon a lotus leaf.

MAMA QUILLA ∽ Besides being a marriage goddess, Mama Quilla is an Incan moon goddess. As such, she was associated with calendars.

Three

MOTHERHOOD

For the womb has dreams.
It is not so simple as the good earth.

— ANAIS NIN

Mother moon, mother earth, mother time, mother nature, great mother of us all....

By these names and more has the Divine Feminine been invoked. It comes as little surprise that so many of the nurturing, loving qualities associated with the goddess are the same required of mothers everywhere.

And as there are experiences of motherhood, so are there goddesses. Each within this section offers us stories and rituals that range from the giddying miracle of new life to the difficulties when a grown child leaves home.

Yemana, the Cuban Santeria goddess of the Caribbean Sea, is invoked by hopeful mothers for aid in conceiving. Expectant mothers of ancient Rome trusted Juno, the great mother goddess, to watch over them as they gave birth, while the Egyptian goddess Renenet helped protect the newborn child by blessing its name. The Australian aboriginal goddesses known as the Wawalak offer an example of the

strength of mothers. Finally, grieving Demeter shows us the commonality of women's sorrow when a child departs the nest.

Most mothers would agree that the patience and skill of a goddess is needed to successfully raise a child; many would also agree that motherhood is perhaps the most rewarding of the many roles offered to us in our lives. Whether we choose to give birth to a child of our own, adopt, or help another with their child rearing, nothing is more goddesslike and all-encompassing than motherhood.

Yemana

THE WATERS OF LIFE

THE WATERS THAT NURTURE NEW life within a woman's womb are a microcosm of the fertile, life-giving ocean ruled by Yemana, Holy Queen Sea. This graceful Cuban Santeria goddess reigns over fertility and motherhood; moon, sea, women — the eternal cycles of life — all fall under her domain. To please the goddess, many of Yemana's devotees choose to wear beaded necklaces as ethereal as irridescent moonlight upon the deep, deep blue of the mother sea.

The shells and creatures of the ocean's depths are also ruled by Yemana. From time immemorial, seashells have been credited with mystical powers. Used in rites of wedding, farming, and death, their graceful curves and enigmatic interior spaces are like women themselves. They symbolize our sexual, regenerative powers as well as the life-giving forces of the ocean and moon.

Like the Virgin Mary, Yemana is often invoked by women who desire a child and are having difficulties with conception. For when a child is born of the waters, arriving like a beautiful pearl from an oyster shell, who can deny the power of Holy Queen Sea?

✦

∽ RITUAL FOR YEMANA ∽
To Conceive a Child — A Fertility Spell

The Santeria religion was developed by the enslaved Yoruba, brought from their native land to Cuba to work on sugar plantations. Since the Yoruba were not allowed to practice their native beliefs, they camouflaged their rituals with the symbols of the Roman Catholicism that was forced upon them; one example of this is the affinity of Yemana to the Virgin Mary. By doing so, the Yoruba remained loyal to their *orishas*, or gods and goddesses, as well as avoided detection and punishment.

This ritual to invoke Yemana's help for conceiving a child uses a pomegranate, a fruit associated with Mary as well as Persephone, the Greek goddess of the underworld. It also represents the future mother's ovaries.

On the first day of your menstrual cycle, buy a beautiful, ripe pomegranate in honor of Yemana. Cut the fruit in two and paint both halves in honey. The sweetness of honey symbolizes the sweetness of life and love; its stickiness symbolizes the ability to attract and hold your heart's desire.

Next, write your name on a piece of paper and place it between the two pomegranate pieces. As you place the two halves of the fruit together, with the piece of paper in the center, concentrate and ask the goddess Yemana to help you become a mother. Say aloud, "May I be as fruitful as your pomegranate is rich in seeds."

To finalize this ritual, light a candle as blue as the sea to honor Yemana. Burn your candle a bit each day until the first day of your next period — if you have one.

This spell was adapted from the work of Migene Gonzalez Wippler.

Juno

MOTHER MOON

JUNO, THE GREAT ROMAN mother goddess, has long been associated with the moon. From earliest times, that luminous orb was believed to magically influence the growth of crops, the behavior of beast and human, the ebb and flow of the sea — and the fertility of women.

Juno, when honored as Juno Lucina, was thought to protect expectant mothers as well as help their babies grow to be healthy. The title Lucina related to the belief that the light of the moon made the child grow within the womb, like a seed within the dark earth; the title Lucina also revealed the trust women placed in the goddess to aid the unborn child to be born. While all aspects of women's lives were important to Juno, paramount was their ability to conceive and give birth to children.

Juno was invoked by young couples yearning for children as well as by mothers laboring in childbirth. They believed she would shield them from many dangers or illnesses. It is perhaps for this reason that Juno is honored as the Preserver and Queen of Mothers.

❋

⌐RITUAL FOR JUNO⌐

The Matronalia — Creating a Shrine for an Expectant Mother

Juno Lucina, Queen of Mothers, was honored every year on March first in a festival called the Matronalia. Women from all over journeyed to her great temple on the Esquiline in Rome. This was a time for women to join together and share stories of their experiences as matrons, mothers, and women. In the goddess's aspect as Juno Moneta, Juno was believed to rule over money and adminstration. Thus, bright offerings of money, which the women took from their husbands, would be left at the goddess's shrine to honor her and win her favor.

To honor Juno, and to invoke her protection of the child growing within you, you could create a shrine to Juno that reflects the imagery of the Matronalia. Shrines are a wonderful way to create power centers, which you can use to focus your energies. They are places that remind us of our deepest, most sacred intentions.

Find a small, quiet surface in your home where you can place several objects that are sacred or special to you. It might be a window ledge, the corner of a shelf, or a small table. Especially good is a spot that gets touched by moonlight. A small mirror placed there could reflect those lunar rays onto you; it was believed that moonlight falling upon a pregnant woman would help her fetus grow as bonny as the moon. Mirrors also symbolize the powers of the moon, the fertility of water.

Peacock feathers, whose decorative eyes represent the all-seeing eyes of the Preserver as she protects women, can be a nice addition to your shrine. Lilies and cowrie shells reveal the fertile, protective powers of Juno also.

Finally, like those Roman matrons of long ago, leave Juno Lucina an offering of a few shiny coins upon your shrine; this simple action connects you with your female ancestors who also yearned, like you, for a healthy, happy child. As you await your child's birth, visit your shrine whenever you feel excited, nervous, or fearful, and see what strength you gain from, Juno Lucina, Queen of Mothers.

❧ OTHER GODDESSES ❧

MUT ❧ Often seen in the form of a woman's body with a vulture head, Mut was believed by the ancient Egyptians to help mothers give birth to children with sound bodies.

SAR-AKKA ❧ In Scandinavia, this Saami goddess helped open the womb for the laboring mother as well as create the fetal flesh within it. After the birth, Sar-akka was invoked in a ritual to predict the little one's future. This powerful goddess was also believed to have created the world.

Renenet

NAMING THE BABY

AFTER THE LONG NURTURING OF pregnancy comes the experience of childbirth. Egyptian mothers of ancient times invoked Renenet, goddess of birth, during this powerful time. She was responsible for creating the baby's desire to suckle its mother's milk, essentially the same as granting it life. But perhaps most importantly, Renenet granted the child its *ren*, or soul name — the secret name that animated it outside the womb.

This soul name could only be bestowed on the child by its mother. In addition to protecting the newborn baby from harm, the magical sound of this name held within its syllables the child's future. It also revealed the framework of the child's personality and place in the world. This special name was kept secret; for an enemy to discover it was an opportunity to gain power over the name-bearer.

As the goddess of childbirth, Renenet was honored as the Goddess of the Double Granary. This refers to the twin nurturing forces of milk and grain, both needed to raise a healthy child. In ancient art, the goddess was often depicted as a woman with the head of a lion or serpent; the Egyptians believed these animals had divine powers, like Renenet herself.

❧ RITUAL FOR RENENET ❧
Naming the Baby — A Ritual

After the baby is born, after the mother's last push propels it toward its first breath of life, wonder and awe sets in. Who is this beautiful child, so wrinkled from womb water, so red with the blood of birth?

Though most mothers choose their baby's name before birth, many times this decision is not finalized until meeting the child outside the womb. Above all, the name of a child defines who he or she is. It is an expression of the child's divine energy. Renenet, the goddess of new babies and soul names, can help new mothers connect with this mysterious newcomer to learn his or her true name — the name that will reveal the child's true nature and protect it as it goes through life.

Even if you've already chosen a name for your new baby, another name could be chosen. This special name, not for daily use, should be kept secret from all but your partner and, when old enough to understand, your child. In many ways, the choosing of this name bears similarities to the confirmation ritual in the Catholic Church: to connect with the special strengths of a particular saint, children add the saint's name to their own when they reach a certain age.

For your naming ritual, choose a time when you can be alone with your baby. As an offering to Renenet, place grain upon a plate and milk in a cup. To focus yourself, light a candle. Be certain to put it on a safe surface away from you and baby — you don't want any worries to distract you during your ritual.

Try to still your thoughts. Look inside your mind. It should be as calm as Egyptian sand — silent, smooth, untouched by wind.

Sit quietly with your new baby. Look deeply into his or her eyes. What do you see? Can you hear the child's true name coming from within? What does it say about the child and who he or she is?

When you have your answer, say your baby's soul name aloud for the first time. Consescrate it by dabbing some milk and a smudge of grain upon your child's brow.

Finally, give thanks to Renenet for your beautiful, healthy child.

∽ OTHER GODDESSES ∽

AJYSIT ∽ This birth goddess, worshipped by the Yakut in Siberia, was believed to relieve the pain of mothers in labor. She visited the family only during the birth of the child. Ajysit was also responsible for the new baby's soul.

HAUMEA ∽ Haumea, a Polynesian and Hawaiian fertility goddess, was believed to have taught women how to give birth by pushing their children from between their legs. She is also known as the mother of Pele, the Hawaiian fire goddess.

The Wawalak

MOTHER STRENGTH

THE DRAMATIC STORY OF THE Wawalak, a pair of sister Australian aboriginal fertility goddesses, demonstrates the mighty love and strength of mothers everywhere.

In the mythical dreamtime, when gods and goddesses wandered the land, the greatest deity of all was the great Rainbow Snake, Yurlungur. Yurlungur created the precious rain. She was honored as the Great Mother and Father and lived in her sacred water hole. But the Wawalak accidentally polluted Yurlungur's water hole with blood from their womb after giving birth.

In response, torrents of rain fell from the sky upon the women and their infants. Water flowed from the hole, threatening to sweep them away. The Wawalak held their babies tightly and covered them with their bodies. They sang and sang to appease the Rainbow Snake's anger. But the instant the sisters rested to gain breath, great Yurlungur arose from the water hole, swallowing the goddesses and their babies whole.

But not even a powerful deity like Yurlungur could undermine the mother strength of the Wawalak. They and their children were reborn of the Rainbow Snake, and they lived again.

❋

∾ RITUAL FOR THE WAWALAK ∾
The Strength of Mothers — A Guided Meditation

The Kunapipi, an aboriginal cult, celebrate the miraculous rebirth of the Wawalak with an elaborate ritual incorporating dances that reenact their story. This fertility ceremony celebrates the return to the womb (symbolized by the Rainbow Snake) and the birth-giving powers of women (symbolized by the goddesses).

Two women are chosen to play the part of the Wawalak sisters and are painted with ochre, a bloodlike pigment. During this ritual, the women are ceremonially reborn from Yurlungur.

The Kunapipi also believe that in the beginning women knew every divine secret and owned all sacred objects — and the special knowledge these items gave to their owners. Later, men stole them away to undermine women's powers. For women who feel overwhelmed and question themselves as they undergo the tests of motherhood, this story reassures us that we already have the wisdom we need within ourselves.

Unfortunately, so much of the world and its frantic demands can steal away our confidence in this. But all we need is to create a condition that allows our trust to be reborn — like the Wawalak from the Rainbow Serpent.

To help create the conditions necessary for you to trust your own strength as a mother, take a quiet moment away from your children to recharge yourself. Close your eyes. As you sit and feel your breath go in and out, feel yourself become calmer.

Try to see before you a great, red landscape. The sky is blue. The land around you is stark but beautiful, populated with dramatic, moonish rocks. As you sit here, feel a warm energy tingling at the base of your spine. As the energy climbs up your spine toward your head, it becomes a serpent striped with all the colors of the rainbow. It surrounds you but it does not threaten or hurt you. Yurlungur, the Rainbow Serpent, has emerged.

Eventually, when you have received the strength you need from Yurlungur, let the energy retreat from where it came — back into your spinal column, down to its base.

When you're ready, open your eyes. Like the Wawalak, you are reborn — and ready to mother again.

↬ OTHER GODDESSES ↬

ROHZENITZN ↬ This beautiful reindeer goddess, honored in Siberia, was believed to be responsible for the fate of newborn infants.

SAULE ↬ Saule, a generous sun goddess, was honored in Lithuania. In addition to helping mothers with childbirth, Saule was also a goddess of weaving, spinning, and other household affairs.

Demeter

THE EMPTY NEST

IN THE JOY OF CREATING new life, it is difficult to think how the act of giving birth to a child also begins its separation from its mother — each day as the child grows, it learns skills which enable it to live on its own. The story of Demeter, the Greek goddess of the harvest, has offered consolation through the ages to mothers struggling with separation from their children.

Demeter's love for her daughter Persephone was so great that the two were inseparable. When Persephone was abducted by Pluto, the god of the underworld, to become his bride, Demeter wandered to the ends of the earth in search of her child. Grief and anger overwhelmed the goddess. So that the earth might reflect her sorrow, she halted all corn and plants from flowering and ripening.

For the first time, winter came, cloaking everything with snow and ice. Humans began to starve from lack of food. Finally, to appease Demeter, Zeus agreed to allow Persephone to return to her mother, as long as she had not eaten while she was away. But Persephone had eaten — several seeds of the pomegranate had passed her lips, this act symbolizing her acceptance of adulthood and sexual maturity. As a compromise, Persephone was allowed to remain on earth with her mother for six months of the year, but she had to spend the rest of the year with her husband.

Not only does this myth explain the origin of the seasons, it also offers us hope. The winter of sadness and deprivation will pass. Spring will arrive again, if we are patient and allow ourselves time to mourn.

✾

∾ RITUAL FOR DEMETER ∾
Undergoing the Thesmophoria — A Group Ritual

Besides the Eleusinian mysteries (see page 28), the greatest ritual associated with Demeter was the Thesmophoria. Called "the festival of sorrow" by the Boeotians, the Thesmophoria was celebrated by married women and mothers each October. As a reenactment of Demeter's grief over her separation from Persephone, this ritual of mourning and catharsis gave women a chance to express difficult feelings associated with motherhood and marriage. For many, it also allowed them the only chance they had all year to leave their homes and family responsibilities to spend time with other women.

The rituals of the Thesmophoria took place over a period of three days. Like the Eleusinian mysteries, these rituals were conducted in secret. By participating in the Thesmophoria, women felt that Demeter would understand their sorrows and, consequently, they would be comforted by her acceptance. Each of the three days corresponded to the dark passage of the moon as it moves from waning to waxing in its cycle.

On the first day of the ritual, Kathodos ("downgoing") and Anodos ("upcoming"), women sacrificed pigs and tossed them, along with figures made of wheat and flour depicting humans and serpents, into a serpent-filled hole. From that hole, they also drew up remains from the previous year's sacrifice and mixed them with seed corn. Some scholars believe that this sacred mixture was used by the women for religious objects. It was on the second day, Nesteia ("fasting"), of the Thesmophoria that the women gave forth to the full range of their grief. As they fasted, they wept and expressed the pain so like what Demeter must have experienced. They also shared pomegranates. The name of the final day, Kalligeneia ("fair-born"), suggests the catharsis that such a display of group emotion must have given these women.

While many women sail through their adult child's departure from their home, for others it is not so easy. For these women, the structure of the Thesmophoria offers a chance to work through the pain of separation while supported by a trusted group of women. Far too often in our society, women are told to swallow their sorrow and get on with life. The Thesmophoria lets us honor our grief and recognize its goddesslike divinity.

To perform this ritual yourself, set aside two nights and a day in a row, preferably ones that coincide with the new moon. Invite your closest friends, the ones able to accept your emotions, to share this time with you. If you can, plan nothing else for these days — no responsibilities, no phone calls.

The first night of your ritual, create a sumptuous feast to share with your friends. At this feast, set a place for your absent child and put food upon it for him or her. Reminisce about the child and your experiences. Try not to give in to your pain about your child's leaving — that territory is reserved for the next night of your gathering. If you can, try to fast after your communal dinner until the second night.

It is on the second night that you must give in to your most difficult feelings. Let the tears flow. Allow your friends to comfort you. Feel their concern, love, and support as you express your sorrow and confusion over what has happened to you. If you are unable to let go, accept it. Talk about it. When you feel the storm of your emotions weaken, break your fast with pomegranate juice.

The last day marks the start of your new life as a mother — the mother of an adult child. Get out of the house and look at the trees and landscape around you as you walk with your friends. You, your friends, and your child are all part of the complex arrangement we call the world. If you feel ready, discuss your plans for your new life: What do you want to do now that your responsibilities have lessened? What will your new relationship with your grown child be like? How will it change?

Remember, like Demeter, you have survived the winter of your sorrow; even if you cannot see the buds of spring, eventually they will come and bring new life.

ᔆ OTHER GODDESSES ᔆ

ABEONA ᔆ Originally worshipped as the Roman goddess of departures, Abeona protects children as they leave their home to enter the world.

Four

CREATIVITY

*Bestower of intelligence and success,
O goddess, bestower of worldly enjoyment and liberation….*

— MAHALAKSHMI STOTRAM

From time immemorial, women have always had a special connection to the creative spirit. When we give way to that connection, we are as powerful as any goddess. They are the unequivocable yes to a world that so often says, "No, you can't." For it is art that lifts our spirits and reminds us of the grand connection between us and the universe that created us. Through the courage of our artistry we can move others to acknowledge our common humanity as well as our divinity.

The goddesses here present many facets of feminine creativity. Athena, the Greek goddess of wisdom, is too often associated with her warrior aspect instead of her original role as the patroness of craftspeople and artisans. Beautiful Sarasvati, the Hindu goddess of music, scholarship, and art, shows the refinements of civilization. The Celtic goddess Brigit was invoked by poets for inspiration. Lakshmi expresses the creativity involved with creating prosperity. And Vesta, the Roman goddess of the hearth, shows us the importance and value of home.

Whether we show our creativity through the medium of paint, words, music, or home, all acts of creativity are ultimately expressions of hope and beauty — and of the Divine Feminine.

Athena

THE WISE ARTISAN

WHAT WOULD OUR LIVES BE like without the gifts of weaving, architecture, and pottery? The great goddess Athena is the creator of all of these arts and many more that give so much to our lives. Worshipped as the mother of wisdom and mother of art, her aspect of Athena Ergane (or Athena "Workerwoman") was called upon as the patroness of spinning and weaving — potent handicrafts associated with women's sacred work as the weavers of fate.

The unusual circumstances of Athena's birth served to foretell of her great intelligence: Unlike other deities, Athena was born fully grown from Zeus's brow. Instead of marrying, she chose to devote herself to wisdom and art, avoiding the romantic intrigues of the rest of the gods and goddesses.

A goddess of peace, goddess of art, wisest of all, too many still know only of Athena's ability to wage war for the defenseless instead of her championship of the creative arts. It was for these powers — not as a warrior — that she was first valued as a goddess throughout the ancient world of the Greek Isles.

⚬ RITUAL FOR ATHENA ⚬
Celebrating Creativity — An Art Ritual

Today, many women associate Athena's wise creativity with career aspirations rather than artistic aspirations. While careers often allow room for the creative, it is important to express our creativity and artistry outside the workplace as well. Luckily, the story of Athena, goddess of wisdom and strength, giver of arts and crafts, offers us the courage to express our creativity, to pursue any latent talents we might have without fear of criticism, whether that critical voice comes from ourselves or others.

Each year in ancient Greece, to celebrate their own creativity as well as to honor Athena's, the girls and women of Athens worked together to weave, sew, and embroider a new *peplos*, or woolen robe, for the statue of Athena housed in the Parthenon. This *peplos* incorporated scenes from Athena's myth and was woven of rich colors; it was begun nine months earlier at the Chalkeia, a celebration dedicated to Athena Ergane and Hephaestus, the god of metalwork and forging.

If you are shy about expressing your creativity, you could use this ritual to Athena as an opportunity to open up to that dynamic side of yourself. Like those women of Athens dedicated to Athena Ergane, goddess of artisans, you could allow Athena to move you to fashion a divinely inspired robe for yourself.

Don't worry if you don't know how to sew. Instead, purchase a ready-made shawl or scarf. Or use a length of fabric, or whatever is available, as long as it makes you feel like a goddess. Decorate it with beads, sequins, other pieces of fabric, and other objects. To attach items, use fabric glue. You could also apply fabric paint or dye.

What would you like to see upon your robe? You could include images sacred to

Athena, such as owls (representing her divine wisdom), serpents (symbolic of feminine divine energy), and the olive tree, Athena's special gift to the city of Athens. Or you could choose to draw images that personally inspire you.

Don't worry about making something you will have to wear in public, nor do you have to show anyone what you are making; thoughts of successful outcome are a sure way to dry the river of inspiration. This ritual to Athena is an opportunity for you to explore what it feels like to be creative without any pressure.

When you are finished, put your *peplos* aside. It is to be worn only when you need Athena's creative energy to jump-start your own.

∽ OTHER GODDESSES ∽

IX CHEBEL YAX ∽ Ix Chebel Yax was honored by the Mayan as an educator who taught women the arts of weaving, basket making, and other art forms. She was thought to be the daughter of the moon.

ZHINU ∽ Like Athena, this Chinese goddess is the patroness of weaving. Zhinu is responsible for making the grand robes worn by the Heavenly Emperor and his family. She is also associated with the stars.

Sarasvati

THE WORD AND ITS SONG

IN INDIA, THE BENEVOLENT goddess Sarasvati is honored for her wisdom and many talents. Her grace and beauty are reflected in her name, which translates as "the flowing one"; this name also refers to Sarasvati's dual aspect as a water goddess who rules over a river that bears her name.

As the personification of all knowledge and education, Sarasvati is credited with creating the Sanskrit alphabet and mathematics. All of the arts and refinements of civilization fall under her wide-reaching domain. This wise goddess of music, language, and scholarship is actively worshipped in many areas of Hindu life. University students perform ceremonies to her before taking examinations. Film directors invoke her help before beginning production on a new film. Musicians praise her with song; the music of the *vina*, an Indian lute, is especially sacred to Sarasvati.

Sarasvati's pure white form and garments are said to be as brilliant as the light of knowledge. They are able to banish all forms of ignorance and bring education to anyone wise enough to desire her enlightening presence.

∽ RITUAL FOR SARASVATI ∽

Invoking Wisdom — A Shrine

Beautiful Sarasvati, as dazzling white as the swans that circle her lotus-blossom throne, is invoked by scholars yearning for her divine wisdom. She is a well-loved goddess in India to this day.

To please Sarasvati and to invoke her wisdom within yourself, create an offering for the Flowing One. Make a shrine by placing four perfect white candles upon a flat surface, one for each direction of the earth. These candles show the goddess's all-pervasive power over the world as well as her four arms, which symbolize the different branches of knowledge.

As you light the candles, bow to each direction. This traditional prayer can be said to welcome Sarasvati's brilliant intelligence into your home:

> *O goddess Sarasvati, white as snow or the moon or the kunda flowers,*
> *clothed in white garments, holding a magnificent vina,*
> *seated on a white lotus and ever gloried. . . .*
> *Protect us from all forms of ignorance.*

As you look at the glowing candles, consider how the light of education brings so much to our world. Consider what it is you need Sarasvati's help with: What projects are you working on that could use her divine spark of understanding and knowledge?

When you are finished, offer Sarasvati a blossom as perfect as her goddess-self, and place it upon your shrine.

Brigit

THE FIRE OF INSPIRATION

THE BURNING FIRE OF INSPIRATION is one that all writers and poets yearn to experience. Celtic people of long ago entreated Brigit, the Celtic goddess, for this divine gift that makes mere words take flight to become art. On the Scottish Isles, Brigit was often seen in the form of a beautiful white swan, as elusive as inspiration itself.

Wise Brigit was thought to be a triple goddess, with each aspect of her divinity bearing a special function. As Brigit, goddess of poetry, poets asked her to take possession of their imaginations to bring forth poems capable of moving people to tears and laughter. Second, Brigit, the goddess of smithing, taught humans the important craft of forging iron, allowing them to create tools to aid their work; perhaps as a reflection, some believe her name translates as "the fiery arrow." Finally, Brigit, the goddess of healing, shared her sage knowledge of herbs to help heal the ill and soothe pain.

The goddess Brigit proved to be so popular and powerful that she is still worshipped today as Saint Bridget. Unable to do away with her, the Catholic Church transformed her miraculous powers into miracles worthy of canonization.

❖

∞ RITUAL FOR BRIGIT ∞

Invoking the Muse— An Imbolg Ritual

Brigit's sacred holiday, the feast of Imbolg, is observed the first of February. It is a celebration that welcomes the return of light from the dark winter. It also marks the start of lambing season and the new life and new year that arrives with spring's start. For this holiday, bards and poets were given special bells to tie to their walking sticks; perhaps these bells were a way of giving recognition to those who had received genius from the goddess.

Many rituals were performed at Imbolg to win the favor of Brigit for the upcoming year. In Scotland, on the night before Imbolg a sheaf of oats would be dressed up and placed in a basket next to a thick wooden club. This basket, called Brigit's Bed, was laid in the hearth and allowed to burn by the women of the household. It was believed that Brigit had chosen to bring good fortune to that home if an impression in the shape of the club was left in the hearth the next morning. People also attempted to prophesy by spreading ashes upon their hearth, later looking to see if the goddess had left her footprint.

To receive the inspiring wisdom of Brigit, the goddess of poets, hang a white wool cloth outside on the eve of Imbolg. By the next morning, when you fetch the cloth, it will have absorbed the energy of the goddess. Set it in a special place for a time when you feel dull and in need of inspiration.

To use this sanctified cloth, before bedtime light several golden candles to invite Brigit's sacred element of fire into your home. As you sit in the candlelight, consider what it is that you need inspiration for. Write it down. Sit for another minute and let your mind empty. When you feel sufficiently relaxed, douse the candles and ready yourself for sleep.

Place the paper with your written request and a pen beside your bed; fold the white cloth under your pillow. As you sleep, the magical energy of Brigit will provide you with your answer. Just be ready to write it down when you wake.

∽ OTHER GODDESSES ∽

THE MUSES ∽ Invoked by poets, artists, and any in need of inspiration, these nine goddesses presided over the arts in the Classical world. As such, each Muse concerned herself with a different area, such as poetry or singing, drama or healing. They were worshipped with libations of milk, honey, or wine poured upon the earth.

SOPHIA ∽ In the ancient Near East, wise Sophia provided humans with the knowledge needed to create literature and the arts. In later years, she was associated with the Holy Spirit in Gnosticism.

Lakshmi

WORLDLY PROSPERITY

CELESTIAL LAKSHMI, THE HINDU goddess of fortune, offers the promise of prosperity and beauty to all. As the divine manifestation of all forms of wealth, she is perhaps the most popular of all the gods and goddesses in India. Perhaps to support this belief, Lakshmi is often depicted upon coins as bright as the fortune she offers.

Indian mythology says that Lakshmi was born of the great Ocean of Milk. As she rose from its depths upon her lotus flower throne, elephants bathed her with water poured from golden vessels. The ocean dressed the goddess in a wreath of unfading lotuses; jewels as bright as stars wrapped themselves around her plump, graceful arms and neck. So beautiful was the new goddess that any who looked upon her knew instant happiness.

Lakshmi married Vishnu, the Conqueror of Darkness; together they had a son, Kama, who was considered the god of romantic love. The three of them represent the golden promise of wealth the world can offer us, if they choose to honor our homes with their blessings of abundance.

❈

❧ RITUAL FOR LAKSHMI ❧
Creating Prosperity — A Divali Ritual

Creating prosperity can be as creative an act as any artistic endeavor. Lakshmi, the goddess of abundance and fortune, shows us how wealth can be divinely inspired.

To honor Lakshmi's prosperity-producing powers, the festival of Divali is celebrated every November on the night of the new moon. Households across the land are made bright and clean. Tiny clay lanterns brilliant with light line roofs, doorways, and window ledges. All this is done to attract the observant eye of Lakshmi — since Lakshmi loves shiny, glittering things, it is thought the more sparkling the home the more likely she will visit it with her blessings.

To invite Lakshmi to visit your home, buy a green candle; green symbolizes fertility and wealth. Write your name upon it and set it in a safe place where it will not be disturbed. Take a flower-based perfume and lightly coat the candle with a small amount — it is thought that the goddess is fond of perfume — but do not use your candle until the oil has completely dried.

Around your candle, create a shrine of bright, glittering objects to charm Lakshmi. Glass beads, golden coins, even copper pennies will please and attract her eye. Clean and arrange your home so that it will be worthy of her visitation.

Wait until the new moon to light your candle to Lakshmi. As you burn it, try not to have any preconceptions of how the goddess will make your prosperity appear. Know that it will come from a place that will be right, and it will be in the form you need.

Burn a little of your candle each night until the full of the moon. By this time, your candle should be gone and Lakshmi will have smiled upon you.

Vesta

THE WARMTH OF HOME

THE WARMTH OF THE HEARTH symbolizes the sunlike center of the home, the warmth of the emotions that bind us to it. Vesta, the goddess called Hestia in Greece, was invoked as the procreative spirit of that place in ancient Rome. She was believed to be present in the hearth of each household, and she served to sanctify the home with her warm, generous energy.

This bountiful goddess was experienced as a friendly presence who lived within the heart of a flame rather than as a being with a physical body. A few pieces of art from this faraway time depict Vesta as a mysterious, veiled figure — more spirit than flesh and blood.

Vesta was a central figure in the Roman pantheon of gods and goddesses. Families would honor Vesta each day with an offering to their hearth, that place so sacred to her. This offering was believed to bring continuing prosperity to the household. It also helped to create the perpetually renewing bonds of home, which hold people together in warmth and affection.

✦

❧ RITUAL FOR VESTA ❧
The Vestalia — A New Home Ritual

Vesta, goddess of the hearth, shows us the importance of creating a home — a warm, bountiful place where we belong, where we are accepted and protected from the harsher elements of the world. The creative skill of making this haven deserves respect and honor. It is an art sacred to Vesta.

Today, Vesta is perhaps best known for her priestesses, the Vestal Virgins. These women, to whom the title "virgin" meant they had not joined their life with a man, rather than any celibacy, lived at her round temple and were responsible for maintaining the goddess's eternal flame and sacred vessel. Kept within this vessel were water, milk, and wine mixed with fruits and grains, perhaps to suggest the nourishing plenty of the earth. Vesta's flame represented the well-being of Rome; a priestess who allowed it to go out could be beaten as punishment for her mistake.

The Vestal Virgins honored Vesta and her sacred flame every June in a festival called the Vestalia. For this, Roman women brought sacrifices of baked goods to her temple-home; the Vestal Virgins offered cakes of salt cooked upon the temple's hearth.

When creating a new home, it can take a while before we feel we truly "live" there; that is, before we have invested our home with our own spirits. To aid this process, create your own version of the Vestalia.

To welcome Vesta's sacred fire into your new home, soon after you move kindle your oven and bake a simple cake. Put it aside for a time when you can invite friends and family over to help you bless your new home.

During your gathering, light your fireplace, if you have one, or light a bonfire in

your backyard. If you're an apartment dweller, candles are a good stand-in for Vesta's sacred hearth.

To consecrate your home with the goodwill of Vesta, pass your cake around. Have each member of your party break off a piece. Then, as each person casts it into the flame (or places it next to your candles), let them say a wish aloud for you and this new place you now call *home*.

∽ OTHER GODDESSES ∽

ANNAPURNA ∽ Many Hindu believe worshipping this generous goddess helps create food to nourish the whole world. Often honored at harvest festivals, Annapurna is depicted in statues and paintings as sitting upon a grand throne offering food to a small child.

HALTIA ∽ Haltia was believed to rule over houses among the Baltic Finn. This benevolent goddess was thought to be a part of the actual structure of the home, bringing good luck to its inhabitants.

HUCHI-FUCHI ∽ In Japan, Huchi-fuchi is the goddess of the hearth. Her fire is responsible for the creation of food, the warming of the home.

Five

Strength

A roof of cedar branches, pine pillows, bamboo blinds,
If only these could screen me from this world of sorrow.

— Lady Nijo

While the world is not a vale of tears, there are times when it seems more so than others. As strong as we may be, these are the times we need a special strength — the potent strength of the Divine Feminine. The goddess myths and rituals offered here express the strengths of our inner souls as well as our glorious bodies. They show us how to deal with the darkness of life and the shadows within our hearts.

Kuan Yin, the luminous Chinese goddess of mercy, brings hope to difficult situations that may seem overwhelming. The healing of heartbreak is promised by Isis, the great Egyptian fertility goddess. Independent Artemis demonstrates the beauty of our bodies, the beauty of our friendships. Oya, the Yoruba goddess of winds, and the fiery Hawaiian goddess Pele show the transforming power of anger and speech.

For better or worse, life encompasses all experiences, joyful and formidable. And so do these goddesses and their stories.

Kuan Yin

MOTHER OF HEALING

MOTHER OF MERCY, MOTHER OF compassion and healing — all these honorifics describe the beloved Chinese goddess Kuan Yin.

Kuan Yin is believed to have been the daughter of a wealthy, cruel man who desired her to marry for status. Gentle Kuan Yin, in hopes of gaining spiritual enlightenment, disobeyed her father and entered a temple. There, she quickly became known for her kind deeds and compassion. But her father was so angered by her act that he had the girl killed. For her good works while alive, Kuan Yin was brought to heaven where she could enjoy an eternity of bliss.

But as she reached heaven's gates, Kuan Yin heard a cry from below. It was someone suffering upon earth, someone in need of her help. Then and there she vowed never to leave humanity until every last person was free from woe. For this vow, Kuan Yin was transformed into a goddess.

Today the goddess Kuan Yin is widely worshipped. She is believed to heal those sick of heart and body, mothers and children in distress, and even seafarers in storms.

❧ RITUAL FOR KUAN YIN ❧
Invoking Healing — A Ritual

Too often in life, we are overwhelmed by troubles. Sorrow encompasses us — and there is only so much we can do. For those beset by worries or illness, the merciful goddess Kuan Yin is a wonderful goddess to invoke.

Chinese families often have a small statue of Kuan Yin in a quiet spot in their homes; many of these figures show the goddess gowned in white and seated upon a lotus throne holding a small child. At these intimate shrines, flowers, fruit, or incense are placed as offerings.

Many believe that the magical act of saying Kuan Yin's name helps the troubled gain comfort. Others choose to go on pilgrimages to the goddess's temple on the mountain of Miao Feng Shan; to win her notice, they shake rattles and other noisemakers as they pray.

The idea of a pilgrimage to visit Kuan Yin is a wonderful one. It suggests that nature, here personified as Kuan Yin the all-merciful, offers us the healing we need for our troubles in her generous, expansive embrace.

The next time you feel overwhelmed with worries, spend some time in nature. Choose a place that is beautiful and serene; even if you live in a city, a quiet glade of trees is often only a train ride away. Bring with you a small offering of fruit or a flower for Kuan Yin.

When you reach your destination, take some time to walk around. The act of walking suggests the passage of time: Time will pass and so will your problems, as difficult as that may be to believe.

When you find a quiet spot where it is unlikely you will be disturbed, sit and

unburden yourself to Kuan Yin. State aloud what is bothering you and why. She will understand, compassionate goddess that she is. Take your time. Remember, the act of saying Kuan Yin's name aloud is believed to bring peace to even the most troubled of hearts.

When you have finished, leave the goddess your offering — and thank Kuan Yin for her help.

☙ OTHER GODDESSES ☙

HYGEIA ☙ The goddess of health in ancient Crete, she was identified by a serpent. The serpent is a traditional symbol of renewal, suggesting the cycle of disease and healing.

GLISPA ☙ The Navajo of the southwestern United States pay homage to this mysterious goddess of the lower world, who brought them the sacred beauty chant. Glispa taught them the ways of magic and healing, thus imbuing them with the powers of the shamans.

PAJAU YAN ☙ This Vietnamese goddess of healing is associated with lunar eclipses and is often worshipped on the first day of the waning moon. Pajau Yan is also invoked for good fortune and health.

Isis

EASING HEARTBREAK

GIFTED, MAGNIFICENT ISIS, THE GREAT Egyptian fertility goddess, shows us the strength of a woman who loves and the transformative powers of her heartbreak.

When Isis was of age, she married her brother Osiris. They lived in such joyful harmony that all were moved by its beauty. Their days were spent nourishing the world; Isis's powers combined with Osiris's brought forth abundant food from the rich Egyptian soil and the fertile Nile. Their nights were blissful with love; no moon or star could outshine their passion.

Everyone loved Isis and Osiris — everyone except Set, their jealous brother. To bring an end to their idyllic rule, Set murdered Osiris and placed his body in a coffin. In time, around this coffin grew a great tree.

Isis searched everywhere for her lover. When she finally found him within the tree, Set stole Osiris's body away from her. He cruelly cut Osiris into fourteen pieces and scattered them all over Egypt. Undeterred, Isis turned herself into a bird and flew up and down the Nile, gathering each piece of Osiris. When she put them next to each other, using wax to join them, only Osiris's phallus was missing; this Isis formed of gold and wax.

Then, using her magical powers, Isis brought Osiris briefly back to life. And using the magic of their love, she conceived a child of him. That child, the falcon-headed god Horus, grew and thrived — and brought vengeance upon Set for the murder of Osiris.

❀ RITUAL FOR ISIS ❀
Transforming Osiris — A Mourning Ritual

As it has since faraway times, the powerful story of Isis offers strength and hope to women who are heartbroken from the loss of their beloved. It shows how we can create hope out of loss — like Isis's mystical resurrection of Osiris.

In ancient Egypt, the myth of Isis and Osiris was reenacted each year in a great ritual of formal mourning. This ceremony was one of their most important religious rites. It allowed participants to experience the painful emotions of the goddess as she searched for and mourned her husband-brother. They also felt her joy at Osiris's rebirth in the form of Horus, their son.

When heartbreak is not fully acknowledged, it spills into all other parts of life and paints it with darkness. The suffering of Isis as she searched for Osiris up and down the Nile suggests the somber journey we must undergo in order to confront our pain to transform it.

To help transform your grief, mold a small heart — *your* broken heart — from aluminum foil. As you sculpt this talisman, think of Isis and her story; think of your story as well. Put all the sorrow of your broken heart into your effort, along with the wisdom that accompanies it.

Next, fill a small, flat-bottomed bowl with water as salty as tears. Stand a thick, sturdy candle in its center. Light the candle. When a small amount of wax has melted, drip it onto your heart talisman. Imagine the wax putting your heart back together, as it did Osiris's body. As you do this, say:

> *Tears to salt water, wax to metal —*
> *Isis, stop my tears, transform my pain.*
> *Mend my heart to love again.*

Then put out the candle.

Do this candle ritual with your talisman for fourteen nights, replenishing the salt water as needed. At the end of this time, take the wax-covered heart and bury it next to a tree for Isis to find and heal, like she did Osiris. And pour the rest of your salt water over it.

∽ OTHER GODDESSES ∽

SEKHMET ∽ This brave, powerful lion-headed Egyptian goddess was associated with the sun. Sekhmet is also an underworld goddess; as such, she is the goddess of strength, vengeance, and enchantments.

Artemis

WOMAN STRENGTH

ARTEMIS, THE GREEK GODDESS OF hunting and the moon, reveals the physical strength and self-reliance of women everywhere. The moon, which rules over the night and wild beasts as well as women's bodies, shows us the vast compass of Artemis's mysterious realm; she was especially associated with the harvest moon and the winter solstice. As a symbol of her sovereignty, Artemis wore a crown shaped like the crescent moon upon her brow. The shape of this headdress also suggests animal horns.

Artemis was honored as Diana in Rome. Independent and wild, she chose to join her life with no man, and those who did not respect her wishes met with terrible deaths. Instead, Artemis lived unencumbered in the woods, her only companions wild animals and a loyal band of nymphs.

Oak groves and freshwater springs were especially favored by the goddess; many of her temples were located within them. But perhaps Artemis's most famed shrine was in Ephesus. There, a great statue of the goddess depicted her as many-breasted, honoring her ability to nourish all creatures — like the earth itself.

❖

～ RITUAL FOR ARTEMIS ～
The Brauronia — Celebrating Women's Friendships and Wild Women

The story of Artemis is a celebration of women's wildness and physical strengths — and also of women's friendships. Her rituals celebrated these qualities as well; many of them encouraged girls and women to join together and dance wildly in the light of the full moon.

The Brauronia was one of the more important rituals to honor Artemis. To apologize to the goddess for the accidental death of a bear cub by a young girl, Athenian girls danced the *arkteuein*. This dance, whose name translates as "to act the bear," is self-explanatory: By dancing like a bear, young girls were allowed to let loose to their inner wildness, to express their strength and athleticism.

To please the goddess, one cult devoted to Artemis encouraged her followers to let their teenage daughters live like bear cubs. These girls lived in the woods, unworried about appearance or rough manners. This gave them the chance to "sow their wild oats" before rejoining the world as women ready for marriage.

To honor your inner wild woman, collect a group of your women friends for a full-moon Artemis celebration. If you can, go to a quiet forest and dance in the moonlight. You could also use a backyard or quiet park. Feel the strength and beauty of your bodies as you dance. Create your own version of the *arkteuein*. What does it feel like to dance like a bear? What other animals can you dance like? Make as many animal noises as you want. If this makes you laugh, then laugh — celebrations *should* have laughter!

When you have finished dancing, sit with your friends in a circle. Let each of you take a turn to speak about what you appreciate in your friendships with each other.

Oya

THE POWER OF WORDS

THE WIND THAT HEAVES TREES from their roots, that tears roofs from homes, is also the wind we use to speak. This wind, produced by our living breath, creates the words we can use to empower ourselves. In Nigeria, the mighty and mysterious Yoruba goddess Oya rules all this as well as the winding Niger River. A popular goddess, Oya is actively worshipped to this day.

Oya is responsible for sending these winds to warn humans of the approach of her husband, the thunder god Shango. Together the couple live in a copper palace in the sky from where they observe the Yoruba. Those who displease Oya and Shango are certain to receive visits from them in the forms of fires, violent storms, lightning, and overflowing rivers.

Oya is a goddess to be approached with great respect. Valued for her charming but penetrating language, many consider her a patroness of feminine leadership. Because of this, Yoruba women will call upon Oya for the words needed to surmount tricky situations.

❖

~ RITUAL FOR OYA ~
Transforming Words — A Shrine

Many times we find ourselves unable to speak when we most need to. The words that can aid us most do not come to our lips, or we are unable to say them because of our fears and insecurities.

Oya is often invoked by women for help with this problem. Her gift for eloquence can help us learn to speak with wisdom and confidence. With this, we can gain authority over any situation.

In Nigeria, shrines to Oya are set into a corner of a home, the altars for them often molded of packed earth. A covered clay pot is used as a centerpiece. Arranged around it are magical amulets and objects: copper crowns symbolize the copper palace she shares with Shango; a sword represents Oya's power of incisive speech; strands of red, orange, or brown glass beads, buffalo horns, and locust pods also represent the goddess.

To gain Oya's gift for articulate speech, create a shrine to invoke her. Use objects that symbolize the power of women's speech — they could be traditional symbols of the goddess or items pertinent to your life. To especially please Oya, offer small dishes of her favorite foods, eggplant and *akara*, special bean cakes.

Considering how another person would handle our difficult situations can be a good way to see them anew. As you create your shrine to Oya, think about times when you have felt intimidated or unable to speak. If you were a goddess, what would you have said? How would this differ from your usual words?

Place a necklace of red and brown beads upon your shrine to sanctify them with the goddess's energy. Many meditation traditions teach that the area in the center of your

throat is a potent chakra, or energy point; wearing Oya's beads there could help unblock it so you can express yourself more fully. Remember to put them on the next time you need to speak with the authority of a goddess.

∽ OTHER GODDESSES ∽

CYBELE ∽ Originally believed to be from Anatolia, this great Mediterranean earth goddess is often depicted in art from that era riding upon the back of a lion. Strong and powerful in word and deed, Cybele was a war deity as well as a goddess who ruled over cities.

Pele

THE PASSION OF ANGER

SIMMERING, ERUPTING, BOILING OVER, CONSUMING — the language of fire is surprisingly similar to the language we use to describe anger. Like lava from a volcano or a fire within dry woodlands, anger has the capacity to destroy when unchecked. But Pele, the Hawaiian fire goddess, shows us how we can use our anger to create change.

Pele rules over all types of fire, most especially the lava of volcanoes. She is believed to live within the smoldering core of Mount Kilauea, one of the most active volcanoes in the world. The smaller lava formations found around the volcano are called "Pele's tears"; local legend says that ill fortune will visit those foolish enough to steal one of these pebbles from her realm.

Famed for her passionate love affairs as well as her temper, Pele often appears to her worshippers in the guise of an alluring woman as beautiful as the moon. Others say she looks like a terrible hag, with brown flesh as crumpled as coarse lava. Whichever way the goddess chooses to present herself, all agree about her fiery temperament — and her ability to destroy as well as create.

❧ RITUAL FOR PELE ❧
Praising Anger — A Bonfire Ritual

The passion of anger has an urgency that can help us better our lives. Pele's ability to present herself as either a wrinkled hag or a seductive woman suggests the inner turmoil that rage can create within women. It shows the ugliness and discomfort that we feel when we are angry — and that we need to confront.

So often in our society women are criticized for giving voice to anger. A terrible double standard exists between the sexes: A man who speaks up or loses his temper is "authoritative"; a woman, on the other hand, is "emotional" — or worse. Pele's story offers an antidote to these beliefs. She tells us that our anger is not only worthy, it is divine. She tells us that our anger is telling us something, something that we really need to listen to.

To invoke Pele's fiery passion, hold a bonfire for the goddess. Use this as an opportunity for a safe haven to work through your anger. Invite some friends who are interested in exploring these feelings with you. Wear comfortable clothing you can move easily in.

Each of you should bring an object which reminds you of something that infuriates you — something that moves you to blind rage. It could be a personal or symbolic object; regardless, it should be something you're willing to sacrifice to Pele.

To perform this ritual, create a circle with your friends in a large, open, outdoor space. One by one, step to the circle's center and place your object within a pile. As you present it, tell the group how it makes you feel and why.

Do not hold back any words, no matter how out of control they may feel. If you feel your body shake with anger, move with it. Do not repress your emotions in any way. If you want to stomp the ground or scream, go for it. Let Pele speak through you.

When each of you has finished speaking, light the pile aflame. Watch the flames climb to the sky, taking your anger with it. As it burns, imagine Pele's lava transforming all that has enraged you. See what answers she gives you for turning your anger into action. See the flames transform into smoke, into ashes — all sacred to Pele.

∽ OTHER GODDESSES ∽

KALI MA ∽ This Hindu triple goddess in her destroyer aspect is widely worshipped in India. Acceptance of Kali Ma the Destroyer recognizes that life cannot exist without death: to destroy through the passion of anger is to create an opportunity for new growth to come from the old.

Some of the ideas in this ritual are inspired by Marcia Starck and Gynne Stein's book, The Dark Goddess: Dancing with the Shadow.

Six

TRANSFORMATIONS

With beauty above me, I am traveling,
With my sacred power, I am traveling,
Now, with long life,
Now, with everlasting beauty, I live….

— EXCERPT, BLESSINGWAY SONG

After the time of fertility comes the time of wisdom.

The full moon has darkened. It is here that we transform into the all-powerful crone. The crone has seen much and knows much. She knows how life begets death, and death begets life. The eternal cycle of the moon held magically within our bodies shows us all we need to know.

We know we are courageous. We are wise. We are crone, a word thought to evolve from "crown." We are crowned with royalty, crowned with the wisdom of our age and of the goddess.

The goddesses described here encompass the darkness of the underworld to the light-giving circle of the sun. Hekate, the Greek goddess associated with menopause and the waning moon, shows the magical powers midlife offers. The Celtic goddess

Arianrhod leads us into the dark hollows of death and back again. Hsi Wang Mu offers us a taste of the peach of immortality. And the Native American goddess Estsanatlehi, or Changing Woman, shows the promise of eternity in the circle of life.

In a way, all goddesses are about transformations of one kind or another. For just as life is continuously transforming, so are we — wise goddesses all.

Hekate

THE DARK MOON

IN ANCIENT GREECE, HEKATE was honored as the dark one, the mysterious moon goddess who brought visions and knowledge from that watery realm. As the wise crone aspect of the great triple goddess, Hekate symbolizes the dark, or waning, moon — the time when the moon withholds its light before emerging to illuminate the night sky once more. This mysterious phase is thought to symbolize the light held inside all women — the inner light that can illuminate our own lives as well as others.

As goddess of the dark moon, Hekate was affiliated with storms, howling dogs, and willow trees. She is symbolized by a golden key, able to unlock untold riches from heaven and earth.

Often placed at crossroads, many statues of Hekate depict her as a triple-headed elderly woman gazing out onto the three directions of past, present, and future. This image suggests the wisdom, knowledge, and joys that middle-age offers women: Having experienced and seen so much, we can now relax and share our live's fruits with the world.

❖

☞ RITUAL FOR HEKATE ☜

Welcoming the Dark Moon— A Menopause Celebration

For many women, menopause is a rebirth into a richly creative phase of life. No longer responsible for children, no longer afraid of accidental pregnancy, we are free to live for ourselves as we wish. But any rebirth brings with it death — the end of our ability to bear children, the finality of our youth. Both facets of this transformation must be acknowledged. The dark moon and Hekate, its goddess, are inspiring symbols for women undergoing menopause.

In ancient times, women who had ceased their monthly flowing were believed to hold their life-giving powers within themselves, like the moon. They were thought to be creating something powerful with their retained womb blood; they were pregnant with wisdom instead of new life. Valued and honored in their communities, these magical, sage women had skills and powers no younger woman could possess. Like Hekate, they were crones, crowned with the intelligence of their years.

Hekate's festival was held on August 13 each year in Greece. Her worship was performed at the darkest hours of the night, often at places where three roads met. Hekate was also invoked by offerings of food; these rituals were known as Hekate's suppers.

To welcome your arrival into menopause, create a celebratory Hekate's supper. On the night of the dark moon, invite your wisest and best older women friends to share their life stories and menopause experiences.

Try using a pendulum to invoke your past, present, and future. Divination was often performed in the goddess's name. Hekate's circle, a pendulumlike gold sphere containing a sapphire, was swung from a cord for answers to questions posed. Responses were deciphered from the direction and ferocity of movement: a straight up-and-down motion could mean yes; a circular motion, no. Or vice versa.

Set your table with holly. This hardy evergreen symbolizes the stages of life — its white flowers represent death; red berries, rebirth and life; the bright green leaves, the hereafter. Share with your friends goblets of heady wine as red as the wise blood held within your womb.

As you celebrate your menopause, invite Hekate to join your feast. Give the goddess a plate of food and a seat of honor at your table.

∽ OTHER GODDESSES ∽

ISAMBA ∽ This goddess of Tanzania was originally associated with the moon. One folktale relates how she became the creator of death.

THE MOIRAE ∽ In ancient Greece, the Moirae were the three Fates, the spinners of destiny. As such, they were responsible for the creation, preservation, and destroying of life — like so many other triple goddesses honored around the world.

Arianrhod

THE SILVER WHEEL

LIFE AND DEATH ARE ASPECTS of the same state — neither can exist without the other, a duality hard to accept as long as we live and breathe and love. The shifting veil that separates the two was envisioned by the Celts as an eternally turning silver wheel in the sky. The keeper of this silver wheel is Arianrhod, a death goddess who also ruled over the moon and fate.

Mythology tells that Arianrhod was the most powerful daughter of Danu, the great Celtic mother goddess. Like the moon itself, Arianrhod was pale of face and mysteriously beautiful. She was responsible for bringing the souls of the dead to her castle, Caer Arianrhod, in the aurora borealis, or northern lights. It was here that the dead awaited Arianrhod's wheel to turn, bringing them the chance to be born anew and live again.

Others believe that the goddess's castle was located upon a long-forgotten island off the English shore. It is there she and her ghostly handmaidens welcome the dead home from their lifelong journey.

❈

⁓ RITUAL FOR ARIANRHOD ⁓
Samhain — Honoring Death

Samhain, the feast of Arianrhod, goddess of death, is celebrated every October 31. This holiday is better known as Hallowe'en, or All Hallows Eve. It is on this evening that the veils separating life and death are thinnest — and the turning of Arianrhod's silver wheel can be sensed.

Many believe that on this evening spirits of the dead roam the earth to bless or curse the living. To appease them, one old tradition involved leaving offerings of food and wine; some think it is from this that the present-day tradition of "trick-or-treating" has evolved. Samhain is also the gateway to winter, the dark half of the year.

No matter how careful we may be in our relationships, when someone dies, we are often left with the burden of untied loose ends — words we wish we had said, sentiments unexpressed. Samhain presents us with a wonderful opportunity for closure with those who have passed over to death, as well as those we may not be in contact with for whatever reason. It is a good time for the healing of wounds, for contemplating our own mortality.

Next Samhain, before you go to any parties or celebrations, take some time alone. Drape a dark cloth over a table and light a single black candle. Place objects there that remind you of death's goddess, Arianrhod — a small silver wheel, a raven's feather, dead flowers, white bones. Also set a fireproof urn upon your shrine, and gather a sheet of paper and a pencil.

By the light of your black candle, consider those you are separated from, whether it be by body or soul. Let your emotions and thoughts have full range: What do you wish you had said before it was too late? What remains unresolved? What do you miss the most about them? What have you incorporated of their life into yours?

When you are ready, write down your answers. Take your time. For full effect, you may be able to do only one person at a sitting. If needed, you can repeat this ritual on another night when the moon is dark.

When you have finished writing, reread your answers. Now place the paper in your urn and light it. Imagine the smoke from the fire carrying your thoughts to the faraway realm where your loved one has gone.

Watch the fire turn your paper to ashes and then to dust. When they have cooled, take your ashes outside and let Arianrhod's cold wind take them where she will.

∾ OTHER GODDESSES ∾

MAMAN BRIGETTE ∾ Maman Brigette is worshipped to this day by those who practice voodoo. She is the goddess of cemeteries and a goddess of death.

MEBUYAN ∾ In Burma, Mebuyan is the goddess of death and the underworld. It is believed that she creates life and death by shaking the tree of life, as if she is harvesting fruit from a ripe tree.

Some aspects of this ritual were inspired by Janice Broch and Veronica MacLer's book, Seasonal Dance: How to Celebrate the Pagan Year.

Hsi Wang Mu

THE PROMISE OF ETERNAL LIFE

THE FORBIDDEN APPLE OF WISDOM that Eve tasted is the same fruit that has granted immortality around the world from time immemorial. In China, however, peaches are offered instead of apples — delectable, magical peaches that promise eternal life, peaches grown by ethereal Hsi Wang Mu, goddess of immortality.

These peaches, called *p'an t'ao* by the Chinese, were grown in Hsi Wang Mu's enchanted orchard, located in her heavenly realm in the Kun-lun Mountains. Fiery phoenixes and snow-white cranes, birds both associated with long life or health, bring grace and beauty to the goddess's golden palace and celestial gardens as they wander about.

The goddess raises her peaches as devotedly as any mother during the three thousand years it takes for them to grow. When they are finally ripe, Hsi Wang Mu invites all the gods and goddesses to a great feast which includes many courses of delicious, exotic foods. Here, they finally dine of the luscious, ambrosial *p'an t'ao* that brings life everlasting.

∽ RITUAL FOR HSI WANG MU ∾

Feeding Eternity — The Festival of the Moon

Peaches, like apples, are potent symbols of feminine power and sexuality; the sensuous curves within the soft, dimpled flesh of the peach are evocative of our genitals, where all life begins. They symbolize the eternal fruitfulness of the universe.

Chinese wizards acknowledged this power by fashioning their magic wands of peach wood. This force of life was also celebrated during the Festival of the Moon, one of the three great annual Chinese holidays. This festival, which also honors the Chinese moon goddess Chang O, takes place on the full moon of the autumnal equinox. It is a celebration of women and children.

To celebrate the eternal life offered by Hsi Wang Mu, hold your own Festival of the Moon. Invite your friends and their children to your home to watch the moon rise high above the trees into the sky. Serve foods as round and pale as the moon: litchi nuts, rice cakes, or pancakes.

Together, ceremonially cut up several ripe peaches. Before you serve them, have the goddess sanctify them: Place them in the moonlight and let her life-giving rays imbue them with blessings. As you offer these peaches, tell your friends they are tasting of life everlasting — the eternity offered by Hsi Wang Mu.

∽ OTHER GODDESSES ∾

IDUN ∞ The Norse goddess Idun grew the apples of immortality in her western garden. These apples were eaten by the gods and goddesses to retain their youth and beauty.

Changing Woman

THE CIRCLE OF LIFE

CHANGING WOMAN, OR ESTSANATLEHI, IS perhaps the most beloved of the Navaho Holy People. A benevolent fertility deity, she is most often associated with corn, that life-giving grain so many rely on for nourishment. As her name suggests, and like the cycles of the earth, Changing Woman changes with the year; she appears as a young maiden in the spring, but by year's end she reveals herself as an elderly crone. She is also believed to be married to the sun.

Besides making the four directions that mark the earth and its energies, Changing Woman created humans. From white shell, she fashioned our bones and brains; she spun our hair of the profound darkness that existed before life; and from red-white stone she made our differently colored skins.

Changing Woman generously taught humans how to control the elements of nature. Her teachings are presented within the Blessingway, a group of essential rituals and chants she is said to have authored. These rituals honor important transformations in life, including joyous occasions such as weddings and comings-of-age.

∽ RITUAL FOR CHANGING WOMAN ∽
The Kinaalda — Celebrating the Continuity of Life

Like the cycle of life that Changing Woman represents, the Kinaalda honors one of the most important points of a woman's life: her transformation from girl to woman.

The Kinaalda is a major part of the Blessingway rituals. For young women who have just experienced their first menstruation, it is a way for the Navajo to celebrate their maturity. By participating in the Kinaalda, young women are blessed with the generous, life-affirming wisdom of Changing Woman — and readied for their new roles as women in their community.

The Kinaalda is held over a four-day period. The young girl honored is dressed in a special costume and her hair pulled back to evoke the sand-painting depictions of Changing Woman. As if they are molding her character as well as her body, the girl's body is massaged by elder women of the tribe; it is believed that at this time the girl's body is as soft as a newborn's.

Perhaps the most important part of the Kinaalda takes place on the final day. This is when the Alkaan, an immense ceremonial cake, is finally eaten. During the earlier part of the Kinaalda, the corn for this cake has been ground by the young girl. As the Alkaan is baked in a pit, it is sprinkled with ceremonial cornmeal and covered with husks. Singing is heard as it cooks overnight:

> *With beauty before me, I am traveling,*
> *With my sacred power, I am traveling,*
> *With beauty behind me, I am traveling,*
> *With my sacred power, I am traveling.*

To mark the miraculous transformations of women and the cycle of life, gather your favorite women together to bake a communal cake.

Traditionally, the Alkaan cake baked during the Kinaalda represents Mother Earth and is offered to the sun as thanks for its help growing the corn. Your ceremonial cake could also be an offering to the sun as well as an acknowledgment of the wisdom of Changing Woman — wisdom we all hold intuitively within ourselves.

Unlike the Alkaan cake, your cake doesn't have to be several feet wide or roasted in a pit; use any recipe that includes the traditional ingredients of cornmeal, egg, oil, and sweetener.

When you have finished baking this cake with your friends, gather together and take turns breaking pieces from it to feed each other. Remember to leave a piece for Changing Woman — the goddess who teaches of the cycles of life, of the transformation of seed to corn and back again.

⟡ OTHER GODDESSES ⟡

BABA YAGA ⟡ Many of us think of Baba Yaga as an evil witch who eats children, which is how she is often presented in Russian fairy tales. Originally this goddess represented the life cycle, from birth to death.

MYESYATS ⟡ Like Changing Woman, this Slavic goddess ages during the year to reflect the different ages of women. Myesyats is associated with the moon and time.

SOURCE NOTES AND SELECTED BIBLIOGRAPHY

Books are by their nature collaborative ventures: I cannot imagine how I could have undertaken writing *Embracing the Goddess Within* without the inspiration and help of the following books.

Indispensible and comprehensive, Barbara Walker's *The Woman's Encyclopedia of Myths and Secrets*, Martha Ann and Dorothy Myers Imel's *Goddesses in World Mythology*, and Patricia Monaghan's *The Book of Goddesses and Heroines* were supremely helpful to me, especially with the shorter descriptions of the lesser-known goddesses; these books deserve a place in the library of any goddess or mythology enthusiast. For those especially interested in initiation or menstrual rituals, Mircea Eliade's *Birth and Rebirth: The Religious Meanings of Initiation in Human Culture* as well as Judy Grahn's extraordinary book *Blood, Bread, and Roses: How Menstruation Created the World* were particularly inspiring to me as I worked. Grahn's book was also very helpful on the subject of wedding rituals and their inherent symbolism. I must also mention Carolyne Larrington's *The Feminist Companion to Mythology*, Christine Downing's *The Long Journey Home: Re-visioning the Myth of Demeter and Persephone for Our Time*, and Merlin Stone's *When God Was a Woman* — these books are treasures for women everywhere.

Several of the quotes beginning each section of this book were taken from Elaine Partnow's *The New Quotable Woman: The Definitive Treasury of Notable Words by Women from Eve to the Present*, an astonishing collection of women's wit and wisdom. They include the Enheduanna quote (page 5), the fragment of poetry by Sappho (page 25), the poem from *The Confessions of Lady Nijo*, which was translated by Karen Brazell (page 77), and the quote from Anais Nin's *Diaries* (page 43). The excerpts from the Blessingway ritual song (pages 93 and 104) were found in Karen Liptak's *Coming-of-Age: Traditions and Rituals from Around the World*. The excerpt from the *Mahalakshmi Stotram* ("Hymn to Lakshmi") (page 61) is, as far as I could ascertain, a traditional Hindu prayer, as is the prayer to Sarasvati (page 67). The Clarissa Pinkola Estes quote (pages 7–8) is taken from the introduction to Charles and Anne Simpkinson's book, *Sacred Stories: A Celebration of the Power of Stories to Transform and Heal*. Every effort has been made to acknowledge the copyright holders of previously published material.

A selected bibliography follows. I hope these books will inspire you to continue reading about the Divine Feminine and her nurturing, healing influence.

Ann, Martha, and Dorothy Myers Imel. *Goddesses in World Mythology*. Oxford University Press, 1993.

Baring, Anne, and Jules Cashford. *The Myth of the Goddess*. Viking Books, 1992.

Bascom, William. *The Yoruba of Southwestern Nigeria*. Holt, Rinehart, and Winston, 1969.

Beier, Ulli. *Yoruba Myths*. Cambridge University Press, 1980.

Bell, Robert E. *Women of Classical Mythology: A Biographical Dictionary*. Oxford University Press, 1993.

Bierhorst, John. *The Mythology of North America*. Quill/William Morrow, 1985.

Bolen, Jean Shinoda. *Goddesses in Everywoman: A New Psychology of Women*. HarperCollins, 1985.

Broch, Janice, and Veronica MacLer. *Seasonal Dance: How to Celebrate the Pagan Year*. Samuel Weiser, 1993.

Bulfinch, Thomas. *Bulfinch's Mythology*. Signet/New American Library, 1962.

Burland, Cottie. *North American Indian Mythology*. Peter Bedrick Books, 1985.

Campbell, Joseph. *The Masks of God: Primitive Mythology*. Arkana/Penguin USA, 1987.

Carlyon, Richard. *A Guide to the Gods*. Quill/William Morrow, 1981.

Carmody, Denise Lardner. *Mythological Woman: Contemporary Reflections on Ancient Religious Stories*. Crossroad Publishing Company, 1992.

Christie, Anthony. *Chinese Mythology*. Hamlyn Publishing Group, 1968.

Davidson, H. R. Ellis. *Myths and Symbols in Pagan Europe: Early Scandinavian and Celtic Religions*. Syracuse University Press, 1988.

Downing, Christine, editor. *The Long Journey Home: Re-visioning the Myth of Demeter and Persephone for Our Time*. Shambhala, 1994.

Eliade, Mircea. *Birth and Rebirth: The Religious Meanings of Initiation in Human Culture*. Harper and Brothers, 1958.

——. *Images and Symbols: Studies in Religious Symbolism*. Princeton University Press, 1991.

Erdoes, Richard, and Alfonso Ortiz, editors. *American Indian Myths and Legends*. Pantheon Books, 1984.

Frazer, Sir James G. *The Golden Bough: A Study in Magic and Religion*. The MacMillan Company, 1958.

Gadon, Elinor W. *The Once and Future Goddess*. Harper and Row, 1989.

Gimbutas, Marija. *The Goddesses and Gods of Old Europe, 6500–3500 B.C. Myths and Cult Images*. University of California Press, 1982.

Gonzalez-Wippler, Migene. *The Santeria Experience*. Original Publications, 1982.

Grahn, Judy. *Blood, Bread, and Roses: How Menstruation Created the World*. Beacon Press, 1993.

Grant, Michael. *Myths of the Greeks and Romans*. Harry N. Abrams, 1962.

Grimal, Pierre, editor. *Larousse World Mythology*. Hamlyn Publishing Group, 1968.

Harding, M. Esther. *Woman's Mysteries: Ancient and Modern*. Harper Perennial Library, 1976.

Hooke, S. H. *Middle Eastern Mythology: From the Assyrians to the Hebrews*. Penguin Books, 1963.

Ke, Yuan. *Dragons and Dynasties: An Introduction to Chinese Mythology*. Penguin Books, 1993.

Kluckhorn, Clyde, and Dorothea Leighton. *The Navaho*. Doubleday Anchor, 1962.

Kraemer, Ross Shepard. *Her Share of the Blessings: Woman's Religions Among Pagans, Jews, and Christians in the Greco-Roman World*. Oxford University Press, 1992.

Larrington, Carolyne, editor. *The Feminist Companion to Mythology*. Pandora/HarperCollins, 1992.

Lehmann, Arthur C., and James E. Myers. *Magic, Witchcraft, and Religion: An Anthropological Study of the Supernatural*. Mayfield Publishing Company, 1985.

Leonard, Linda Schierse. *On the Way to the Wedding: Transforming the Love Relationship*. Shambhala, 1986.

Liptak, Karen. *Coming-of-Age: Traditions and Rituals from Around the World*. The Millbrook Press, 1994.

Locke, Raymond Friday. *The Book of the Navajo*. Mankind Publishing Company, 1992.

MacCana, Proinsias. *Celtic Mythology*. Peter Bedrick Books, 1983.

Monaghan, Patricia. *The Book of Goddesses and Heroines*. Llewellyn Publications, 1993.

Nicholson, Irene. *Mexican and Central American Mythology*. Hamlyn Publishing Group, 1969.

Nicholson, Shirley. *The Goddess Re-awakening*. Quest Books, 1989.

Osborne, Harold. *South American Mythology*. Hamlyn Publishing Group, 1969.

Parrinder, Geoffrey. *African Mythology*. Hamlyn Publishing Group, 1969.

Partnow, Elaine, editor. *The New Quotable Woman: The Definitive Treasury of Notable Words by Women from Eve to the Present*. Meridien Books/Penguin USA, 1993.

Perowne, Stewart. *Roman Mythology*. Peter Bedrick Books, 1988.

Piggott, Juliet. *Japanese Mythology*. Peter Bedrick Books, 1991.

Pomeroy, Sarah B. *Goddesses, Whores, Wives, and Slaves: Women in Classical Antiquity*. Schoken Books, 1975.

Rush, Anne Kent. *Moon, Moon*. Random House/Moon Books, 1976.

Rutherford, Ward. *Celtic Lore: The History of the Druids and Their Timeless Traditions*. HarperCollins, 1993.

Sander, Tao Tao Liu. *Dragons, Gods and Spirits from Chinese Mythology*. Peter Bedrick Books, 1980.

Sered, Susan Starr. *Priestess, Mother, Sacred Sister: Religions Dominated by Women*. Oxford University Press, 1994.

Simpkinson, Charles, and Anne Simpkinson, editors. *Sacred Stories: A Celebration of the Power of Stories to Transform and Heal*. HarperSanFrancisco, 1993.

Spence, Lewis. *The Illustrated Guide to Native American Myths and Legends*. Longmeadow Press, 1993.

Spretnak, Charlene. *Lost Goddesses of Early Greece*. Beacon Press, 1992.

Starck, Marcia, and Gynne Stein. *The Dark Goddess: Dancing with the Shadow*. The Crossing Press, 1993.

Starhawk. *The Spiral Dance*. HarperCollins, 1979.

Stone, Merlin. *When God Was a Woman*. Harvest/Harcourt Brace Jovanovich Books, 1976.

Sykes, Egerton. *Who's Who in Non-Classical Mythology*. Oxford University Press, 1993.

von Franz, Marie-Louise. *The Feminine in Fairy Tales*. Shambhala, 1993.

Waldherr, Kris. *The Book of Goddesses*. Beyond Words Publishing, 1995.

——. *Persephone and the Pomegranate*. Dial Books, 1993.

Walker, Barbara G. *The Crone: Woman of Age, Wisdom and Power*. HarperSanFrancisco, 1985.

——. *The Woman's Encyclopedia of Myths and Secrets*. HarperSanFrancisco, 1983.

——. *Women's Rituals: A Sourcebook*. HarperCollins, 1990.

Wolkstein, Diane. *The First Love Stories*. HarperCollins, 1991.

Young, Serinity, editor. *An Anthology of Sacred Texts by and about Women.* Crossroad Publishing Company, 1993.

SUBJECT INDEX

ABOUT THE AUTHOR

KRIS WALDHERR has written and illustrated numerous books. Her work is perhaps best known from her recent book, *The Book of Goddesses*, which was an American Booksellers Association Pick-of-the-List and a Book-of-the-Month Club selection. Starhawk, author of *The Spiral Dance*, called *The Book of Goddesses* "gorgeously illustrated, beautifully written, and multicultural. . . . Sure to be a classic." It was also praised by Anne Baring, author of *The Myth of the Goddess*, as "an exceptional book — beautifully conceived, written, and illustrated." Another book, *Persephone and the Pomegranate*, was praised by *The New York Times Book Review* for its "quality of myth and magic" and by Jean Shinoda Bolen, author of *Goddesses in Everywoman*, as "a beautifully done retelling of the major mother-daughter myth." Kris Waldherr's strong interest in mythology and folklore, especially women's myths, led to the extensive research which became *Embracing the Goddess Within*.

Kris Waldherr was born in West Haverstraw, New York, and received her bachelor of fine arts degree from the School of Visual Arts in New York City. Her artwork has been shown throughout the United States and Great Britain.